The Paradox of
Philosophical Education

APPLICATIONS OF POLITICAL THEORY

Series Editors: Harvey Mansfield, Harvard University, and
Daniel J. Mahoney, Assumption College

This series encourages analysis of the applications of political theory to
various domains of thought and action. Such analysis will include works on
political thought and literature, statesmanship, American political thought,
and contemporary political theory. The editors also anticipate and welcome
examinations of the place of religion in public life and commentary on classic
works of political philosophy.

Lincoln's Sacred Effort: Defining Religion's Role in American Self-Government, by Lucas E. Morel

Tyranny in Shakespeare, by Mary Ann McGrail

The Moral of the Story: Literature and Public Ethics, edited by Henry T. Edmondson III

Faith, Reason, and Political Life Today, edited by Peter Augustine Lawler and Dale McConkey

Faith, Morality, and Civil Society, edited by Dale McConkey and Peter Augustine Lawler

Pluralism without Relativism: Remembering Isaiah Berlin, edited by João Carlos Espada, Mark F. Plattner, and Adam Wolfson

The Difficult Apprenticeship of Liberty: Reflections on the Political Thought of the French Doctrinaires, by Aurelian Craiutu

The Dialogue in Hell between Machiavelli and Montesquieu, by Maurice Joly, translation and commentary by John S. Waggoner

Deadly Thought: "Hamlet" and the Human Soul, by Jan H. Blits

Reason, Revelation, and Human Affairs: Selected Writings of James V. Schall, edited and with an introduction by Marc D. Guerra

Sensual Philosophy: Toleration, Skepticism, and Montaigne's Politics of the Self, by Alan Levine

Dissent and Philosophy in the Middle Ages: Dante and His Precursors, by Ernest L. Fortin, A.A.

Behemoth *Teaches* Leviathan: *Thomas Hobbes on Political Education*, by Geoffrey M. Vaughan

Gladly to Learn and Gladly to Teach: Essays on Religion and Political Philosophy in Honor of Earnest L. Fortin. A.A., edited by Michael P. Foley and Douglas Kries

Cultivating Citizens: Soulcraft and Citizenship in Contemporary America, edited by Dwight D. Allman and Michael D. Beaty

The Paradox of Philosophical Education: Nietzsche's New Nobility and the Eternal Recurrence in Beyond Good and Evil, by J. Harvey Lomax

The Paradox of Philosophical Education

Nietzsche's New Nobility and the Eternal Recurrence in Beyond Good and Evil

J. Harvey Lomax

LEXINGTON BOOKS
Lanham • Boulder • New York • Oxford

LEXINGTON BOOKS

Published in the United States of America
by Lexington Books
A Member of the Rowman & Littlefield Publishing Group
4720 Boston Way, Lanham, Maryland 20706

PO Box 317
Oxford
OX2 9RU, UK

British Library Cataloguing in Publication Information Available

Library of Congress Cataloging-in-Publication Data

Lomax, J. Harvey, 1948-
 Nietzsche's new nobility and the eternal recurrence in Beyond good and
evil : a paradox of philosophic education / by J. Harvey Lomax.
     p. cm. — (Applications of political theory)
Includes bibliographical references and index.
 ISBN 0-7391-0476-4 (alk. paper) — ISBN 0-7391-0477-2 (pbk. : alk. paper)
 1. Nietzsche, Friedrich Wilhelm, 1844-1900. Jenseits von Gut und Bèose. 2. Ethics.
3. Nobility. 4. Eternal return. I. Title. II. Series.
 B3313.J43 L66 2002
 193—dc21   2002010336

Printed in the United States of America

♾™ The paper used in this publication meets the minimum requirements of American
National Standard for Information Sciences—Permanence of Paper for Printed Library
Materials, ANSI/NISO Z39.48–1992.

Dedicated to Joseph Cropsey,
teacher, free spirit, and friend

Acknowledgments

Warm thanks are due to the Bradley Foundation, the Earhart Foundation, and the Siemens Foundation. They all kindly provided financial or other support.

These formal acknowledgments cannot begin to convey the author's thankfulness to those who have contributed to the present intellectual project, especially to Hans-Georg Gadamer, Joseph Cropsey, and Heinrich Meier. This book is dedicated to Professor Cropsey in deep gratitude and the highest respect.

Werner Dannhauser also served as a rich source of inspiration and encouragement. Over the years, George Anastaplo, Karen C. Armour, Mark Blitz, Christopher A. Colmo, David N. Cox, Jules Gleicher, James D. King, William R. Marty, Mary P. Nichols, Pamela W. Proietti, Paul Ricoeur, Robert L. Stone, Nathan Tarcov, Rudiger Völkel, and Ernest J. Walters provided indispensable stimulation, aid, and comfort.

An eternity might suffice to express proper appreciation for their collegiality and friendship. Then again, it might not.

Contents

Preface

Nietzsche's current fashionableness among scholars and intellectuals owes much to Martin Heidegger and the "post-modernists," most of whom acknowledge or display their indebtedness to him in turn. Postmodernists, though, generally fail, as nearly everyone fails, to distinguish between Nietzsche and his antirationalist, nihilistic shadow. Thus they fall victim to his irony. Few interpreters have noticed that, and in what sense, Nietzsche ultimately came not to bury the love of wisdom in its rags but to revive or resurrect it into a new splendor.

This brief volume is not meant to provide an apodictic, scholarly proof or the last word on Nietzsche. Rather, this study indicates the type of close reading, and especially certain key questions, necessary to a fitting, dialectical confrontation with Nietzsche's new nobility. Hitherto, even the best commentators have neglected to focus on Nietzsche's nobility and follow his esoteric treatment thereof through its most disconcerting, Platonic-Socratic twists and turns. If successful, the following work will serve as a candle for bold spelunkers navigating the darkest tunnels in the Nietzschean labyrinth.

Thereafter, the best explorers will find their way, unassisted, through the rest of the maze and enjoy a glimmer of the almost dazzling radiance of philosophy.

The key to comprehending this somewhat odd, unconventional book is also the key to unriddling Nietzsche himself. The concealed heart of the mature Nietzsche's activity, which evidently no one has ever quite grasped, yet in terms of which everything else can be put into proper context, can be encapsulated in a single sentence. He resurrects religion in a strange new form in order to destroy its seductiveness; shakes philosophy to its eyeteeth, smashes its imposing structures and hallowed doctrines, renders it radically dubious, precisely in order to make it radically possible again; and combines philosophy and religion so as to make clear their insuperable incompatibility. He demolishes constructively, and he joins asunder.

The parts of this study draw their intelligibility from the whole. The reader who halts before the end will, so to speak, comprehend nothing. In the terse, introductory chapter below, the issue comes to light as the agon between philosophy and poetry. The second chapter develops this issue through an extended, passage-by-passage analysis of chapters 1 and 2 of *Beyond Good and Evil*, where Nietzsche critically treats philosophy per se. In this chapter of the book, an attempt is made to indicate what a careful perusal of the aphorisms in context should involve. The third and final chapter, concerning religion, increasingly presupposes that the reader has already completed the close reading and initial considerations. Accordingly, the third chapter proceeds more directly toward crucial questions and reflections. Thus by the end of the book the text is condensed and moves rather rapidly. The circle back to the agon with poetry does close, though as much by systematic adumbration as by explication. Finally, the appendix might shed light on the relation between Zarathustra's seductive poetry and the philosopher's noble soul.

The compactness at the end should offer advantages to Nietzsche's preferred readers, who may find the complete outlines of a deeply unorthodox interpretation from within provocative, but prefer not to have all the dots connected in advance. For "no one can so well understand a thing and make it his own when he learns it from another as when he discovers/invents it himself" (Renè Descartes, *Discourse on Method*, Part VI; cf. first two sentences of Part V). The optimal pattern for such readers would be illumination followed by groping, followed by illumination on a higher plane. Such readers, steeped in Nietzsche's writings and in Plato's, will grasp the utility of intentional exaggerations, jokes, poses, riddles, and red herrings. They will appreciate the value, for thought, of surprising jolts, sudden shifts, and studied silences. If each chapter below concludes, following the author of *Thus Spoke Zarathustra* and

Beyond Good and Evil, with an unexpected turn and paradox, such is the nature of philosophic education.

The venerable works and lectures of Heidegger, Leo Strauss, and Karl Löwith so heavily influenced the interpretation offered here that only a blanket acknowledgment can do them any justice. One might call it my highest aspiration to become a duly grateful and worthy student of them all and hence, as Nietzsche taught, a disciple of none.

Geneva
Summer, 2001

"To cheat oneself out of love is the most terrible deception. It is an eternal loss for which there is no reparation."

—Søren Kierkegaard

Chapter One

Poetry

FOR SWIMMERS IN ICY WATERS

"Why, holy Socrates, do you always adore
This youth? Do you know nothing greater than he?
Why do you look on him
Lovingly, as on gods?"

—Hölderlin, "Socrates and Alcibiades"[1]

Nietzsche can be said to be the intellectual representative par excellence of the crisis of the West. His proclamation that God is dead is the clearest philosophical communication to the great body of ordinary men that chaos has displaced every old metaphysical and moral order. His Zarathustra speaks as a herald's cry for a new age of humanity, which will rise out of the ashes of the old to a hitherto unseen power, glory, and beauty.

Our principal motive for investigating Nietzsche might be regarded as a contemporary or historical concern, our interest in the peculiar crisis of civilization in which we find ourselves. Yet the terms in which Nietzsche frames the issue invite us to view him as a continuer of a very ancient agon, the contest between philosophy and poetry. Nietzsche attacks all previous philosophers in the name of a poetic philosophy or philosophical poetry of the future. He thus does resume the old struggle between philosophy and poetry, even if he is correct in presuming to shift the arena to dangerous, unexplored seas and to open the contest authentically for the first time.[2]

1

The nature of the contest merits a bit of elaboration from the outset. Poetry as self-expressive, inspired genius can appear to offer one means of access to first principles for human life, and philosophy as self-critical, dialectical reflection, another. Yet are there only two possibilities? If revelation is conceived to come only from a deity absolutely external to man, the alternatives to the rule of reason can be said to be at least two: poetry and divine revelation. Admittedly, most philosophers treat revelation and poetry as comprising only one alternative to philosophy as love of wisdom. Nietzsche and the ancients might even agree that poetry offers the only real alternative, for they evidently do not believe in the possibility or reliability of lucid communication by nonhuman gods of nonhuman origin. For their exclusion of a separate berth for divine revelation, however, the ancients can be assailed with the argument that their own eternals are ultimately no more certain than those of revealed religion, and Nietzsche can be challenged on the ground that his human divinity finally does not make sense unless it can be referred to an imperishable god or gods.[3] Moreover, one can reasonably doubt the apodictic disprovability of divinity or of divine miracles. Wherever these reflections may lead us when fully developed, we are not entitled from the beginning to reject poetry, reason, or divine revelation.[4] Keeping the door open to non-Nietzschean divine revelation also has the advantage of receptivity to the manifest teaching of Sören Kierkegaard, who develops the theistic strand of existentialism.

If there are indeed three contending sources of the first principles of human affairs, are there not more? Probably not. Of course many regard the experience of pleasure as the great eureka of life and in fact pursue pleasure. But pleasure does not qualify as a fourth contender, because vulgar hedonism cannot overwhelm truly thoughtful human beings, and loftier hedonism, Epicureanism strictly speaking, collapses into the life of reason. Moreover, although quite a few pursue honor, honor obviously has no independent status as a first principle, because a thoughtful man must face the question of what is honorable—a query that only poetry, philosophy, or divine revelation can answer. Similarly, statesmanship alone cannot provide the first principles, for the statesman requires something transcending mere statesmanship for an answer to the question, What is good life? Nietzsche as champion of poetry has such epochal significance because his genius plumbs the depths in confronting that deepest and most comprehensive question.

What charges does poetry press against philosophy? In the spirit of poetry one might reply not altogether flippantly by playing an overture by Mozart—or by composing one's *own* music, as Nietzsche does in his *Prelude* to a Philosophy of the Future (the subtitle of *Beyond Good and Evil*).[5] The point, in speech, would be that poetry succeeds where philosophy fails in giving beauty and the passions their due. "How little is required for pleasure! The sound of a bagpipe. Without music life would be an error" (*Twilight of the Idols*, "Maxims and Arrows," 33). "In music the passions enjoy themselves" (*BGE* 106). Philosophy might counter with a claim to grant beauty and the passions exactly their due, and would accuse the poets of glorifying the passions to excess. Consideration of the entitlements of beauty and passion would accordingly belong to a comprehensive assessment of Nietzsche. For present purposes it suffices to observe that the poet's likely first criticism of philosophy rests on a moral interpretation of the human economy. Similarly, poetry claims a rhetorical superiority over philosophy that enables the poet to mold human beings more effectively.

The poet will also advance two theoretical justifications of poetry against philosophy. One is the extraordinary claim that the poets understand the world and man's place in it better than do the philosophers. By nurturing a much greater concern for particulars, by developing individuality or selfhood to the fullest, by glorifying in the transitory and even in transitoriness, the poet sees elements of the world that philosophy overlooks or fails to appreciate fully. The poet possesses insights the philosopher may lack, "above all the understanding of men's attachment to the world and what this implies." Even if that claim be granted, the philosopher may retort, a great thinker who became and remained a poet primarily for the sake of the critical understanding of humanity that poetry offers, might be first and foremost a philosopher. The case for poetry has not yet been made.

The other theoretical attack by poetry on philosophy takes us directly into the brief preface of *BGE*. Were *BGE* a philosophical treatise as traditionally understood, the preface might read as follows: "My purpose in this treatise is to expose the dogmatic and therewith untrue character of all previous philosophies, above all of Platonic philosophy with its doctrines of pure spirit, which depreciates the body, and the good in itself, which restricts the power of the human will. I shall replace Platonism with a doctrine of perspectivism and will to power. One can arrive not at the truth but only at one's own truth, which depends not on anything 'objective' but on the structure of each human being's particular self, on one's physiology." If this prosaic statement reflects a sound grasp of the limits of human understanding, genuine philosophy in the old-fashioned sense is impossible. Ultimately one experiences only oneself, as Nietzsche's alter ego observes in *Thus Spoke Zarathustra*. Thus the highest possible attainment of any new philosophy after Nietzsche will be self-consciously poetic. And if one experiences only oneself, the highest human accomplishment will be the fullest development of the self.

At this point the philosopher can find himself hard-pressed to defend himself. Among other things, the poet will demand the source of the philosopher's original premises, which by definition cannot derive from previous arguments. If the beginnings come from common sense, what on earth does that mean, and what testifies to its validity? If the first premises obtain from experience, does not experience involve induction, which is completely reliable neither in principle nor in fact? "There is something arbitrary in [the philosopher's] stopping here to look back and look around, in his not digging deeper here but laying his spade aside; there is also something suspicious about it" (*BGE* 289). Perhaps most gravely, what enables the philosopher to "see" himself so clearly that he restrains his self from biasing his reasoning—can the pristine self be both observer and observed? These are by no means new questions that suddenly arise with Nietzsche, but they are weighty and inescapable.

The above formulation of Nietzsche's purpose in *BGE* egregiously fails to capture the heart of the preface. It constitutes a misleading recapitulation because *BGE* does not even resemble an old-fashioned philosophical treatise directed above all at reaching the pristine truth. As the preface develops, and especially at its end, Nietzsche indicates that his primary interest in dogmatic philosophy does not lie in the opportunity to correct the dogmatists' blunders as seekers after truth. Instead, what counts is that through history the master dogmatist, Plato, has provoked a tremendous crisis in the human spirit that makes possible an uplifting of humanity to awesome new heights. What character will this new breed of men have — whence and how shall they come about, what will they pursue, and what can they be expected to accomplish? From the beginning, Nietzsche addresses these questions in an extremely elusive way. But already in the preface Nietzsche plants in the mind of the attentive reader the suspicion that the true subject of *BGE* might be Nietzsche's new nobility.

In Nietzsche's eyes the history of philosophy so far comprises a series of tragedies. He does portray philosophers so far as having made great buffoons of themselves in sacrificing "for the sake of truth," and in *The Birth of Tragedy* he does complain that philosophic optimism destroyed ancient tragedy. Nevertheless, a pessimistic form of tragedy has been at the real core of philosophy at least since Socrates.[6] Nietzsche intends to transform philosophy so as to extirpate not tragedy per se but pessimism from the heart of philosophy. He wants to make philosophy more Dionysian, more life-affirming. Nietzsche will uplift the best of his readers to such heights of the soul that to them even tragedy will cease to have a tragic effect.

Early in the preface to *BGE* Nietzsche reprimands his philosophic predecessors for "the gruesome seriousness" and "clumsy obtrusiveness" with which they approach truth. Apparently the proper method for winning a woman's heart combines a cheerful insouciance with subtle but masterful conquest. Nietzsche himself, it appears, will be the adept lover, the first lighthearted conqueror of truth in history. Gaiety will supplant pessimism in the philosopher's heart. In the words of Zarathustra, "we should consider every day lost on which we have not danced at least once. And we should call every truth false that was not accompanied by at least one laugh." Nietzsche in *BGE* aspires to be the knight of the cheerful countenance. We cannot leave it at that, however. For hardly has Nietzsche disparaged seriousness before he refers to himself as "speaking seriously," thereby revealing a serious purpose behind his promotion of lightheartedness at the expense of seriousness.

We shall study *BGE* as a work guided by a moral-political intention, a deeply serious intention that never completely loses its grip on the author, not even during his most rapturous songs and high-hearted dances. If our thesis should bear weight, Nietzsche overthrows the philosophers of old not out of uncorrupted love of truth but for the sake of a morality toward which his entire teaching is directed. Accordingly, the doctrine of the will to power will reveal itself as a moral propaedeutic rather than simply a metaphysics in the old sense. Nietzsche appears to give his imprimatur to our hypothesis in paragraph 6 of *BGE*, where he proclaims that "the moral (or immoral) intentions in every philosophy constituted the real germ of life from which the whole plant has grown." A philosopher's so-called philosophy is highly personal, "and above all, his morality bears decided and decisive witness to who he is— that is, in what order of rank the innermost drives of his nature stand in relation to each other." Since reason does not occupy the core of his being, the philosopher is guided by a "morality" grounded only in the fortuitous order of rank of his instinctive desires, not in truth. Yet precisely the supremacy of Nietzsche's moral intention may require him to salvage vestiges of old-fashioned truth in his writings; for, to persuade one's readers and foster their abiding allegiance to one's moral doctrine, must one not convince them of its verity?

The true subject of Nietzsche's principal works discloses itself as a poet's new morality, both lighthearted and serious, a new nobility beyond good and evil. The meaning of that nobility is addressed thematically in *BGE*. The book begins at a rather low point, the prejudices of the philosophers, and moves to a concluding ninth chapter on nobility. (The number of chapters recalls the nine Muses.) Would not even the naive reader assume that such a movement represents an ascent? Although under closer scrutiny a variety of movements and counter movements come to view at different levels, in a significant sense the apparent ascent that we have noticed remains an unbroken one.[7] The first three chapters, "On the Prejudices of Philosophers," "The Free Spirit," and "The Religious Essence" address, roughly speaking, theoretical matters, whereas the last five chapters generally concern morality and politics. In the light of Nietzsche's assertion that morality is the alpha and omega for philosophers, the earlier chapters can appear to serve as handmaidens clearing the way for the later ones. In important respects, this conjecture will be borne out by the text.

The image of a handmaiden clearing the way accords nicely with the aforementioned subtitle of Nietzsche's weightiest prose work, *Prelude to Philosophy of the Future*. The song or symphony proper, a philosophy of the future, does not appear in *BGE*. Somewhat disconcertingly, chapter 9 on nobility is followed by an "Aftersong." Even though it seems impossible for Nietzsche to provide the main musical work, he nevertheless can provide its aftersong. Or could it be that the ostensible prelude is itself the principal piece after all? The Aftersong concludes:

> O noon of life! Second youthful state!
>   O summer garden!
> Restlessly happy and expectant, standing,
> Looking all day and night, for friends I wait;
> For new friends! Come! It's time! It's late!
>
> *   *
>
> *
>
> This song is over—longing's dulcet cry
>   Died in my mouth.
> A wizard did it, friend in time of drought,
> The friend of noon—no, do not ask me who—
> At noon it was that one turned into two . . . .
> Surest of our victory, we celebrate
>   The feast of feasts:
> Friend Zarathustra came, the guest of guests!
> The world now laughs, rent are the drapes of fright;
> The wedding is at hand of dark and light . . . .

There does seem to be reason to doubt that any unwritten philosophy of the future, sung by new friends, can crown Nietzsche's crescendoes in *BGE* and *Thus Spoke Zarathustra*. Zarathustra is the awaited friend, the guest of guests. The aftersong is entitled "From High Mountains: Aftersong." High mountains are the highest place on earth, and since Nietzsche vigorously denies the superterrestrial, what is atop high mountains is the highest simply. Evidently Nietzsche's hopes for the future, as though its philosophers might far transcend himself or Zarathustra, are not nearly so lofty as they first appear.

Nietzsche sets forth on a poetic project that promises to lift human community and the human soul to an unheard of elevation. He proclaims the advent of the superman. If from the outset he regards that promise as unfulfillable—except perhaps insofar as Zarathustra may experience such ecstatic heights in his dithyrambic intoxications— why the trumpets, and why the prodigious effort? Might Nietzsche intend us to think of the most famous of all philosophic-poetic projects with similar promises, likewise disappointed in the end, in Plato's *Republic*? Considering Nietzsche's characterization of Socrates as the vortex of world history, we should not dismiss the possibility lightly, especially in view of the preposterous proposals for human breeding advocated for the aristocracies of both the *Republic* and *BGE*. Despite undeniable differences, Nietzsche's Zarathustra, not unlike the Platonic-Socratic philosopher, does find it necessary to leave the fellowship of the so-called "higher men" and the bad air of his cave. Wherever these parallels might take us, in both authors we should beware underestimating the salutary potential inherent in the disillusioning lesson of the epic failure. A magnificent failure might even point us toward a path to a qualified success. But what do we discover behind the mask of the great visionary poet? A philosopher?

Notes

1. See Martin Heidegger, *What Is Called Thinking*, Part I, Lecture 2.
2. When a succession of false prophets is at last followed by the one true prophet, in a sense the true prophet does continue the tradition of prophecy, even as this real McCoy breaks with the errors of predecessors.
3. To these theoretical complaints on behalf of divine revelation, familiar moral objections can be added. For example, in the absence of fanaticism the generality of men might well fare better believing rather than disbelieving in an immortal God or gods who establish a cosmic order and pronounce judgments on the deeds or souls of mortal humans. If awe of the holy can transfigure and elevate the lives of many faithful, if fears of divine punishments and hopes of heavenly blessings can frequently foster more civil behavior, even nonbelievers can benefit enormously from the fruits of religion. Conceivably such moral considerations, time honored but not necessarily timeworn, could carry more weight than the others.
4. In fairness we would have to consider the psychological grounds for the philosopher's rejection of revelation. (A) At a minimum the philoso-

pher's will resists unquestioning obedience to a perceived tyrant; out of love of his own freedom the philosopher abhors the supposed shackles of faith. (B) That stiff-necked will remains intransigent in the absence of existential desperation or any compelling reason to regard one particular religious metaphysics as true—especially in light of fiercely competing claims among the religions. (C) The philosopher may very well even consider each of the various religious doctrines as radically contrary to nature because internally contradictory and psychically pernicious for development of one's, or at any rate the philosopher's, highest humanity.

5. Hereafter cited as *BGE*. Translations of Nietzsche's writings derive, with occasional emendations, from the Walter Kaufmann editions. On Nietzsche and music one can consult Curt Paul Janz, "Nietzsche's Conception of Music" in Michael Gillespie's edited collection entitled *Nietzsche's New Seas: Explorations in Philosophy, Aesthetics and Politics* (Chicago: University of Chicago Press, 1988), pp. 97–116 and Gillespie, "Nietzsche's Musical Politics," pp. 117–49 in the same volume.

6. See, for example, *Twilight of the Idols*, "Maxims and Arrows" 11, *Gay Science* 340, and *Twilight*, "The Problem of Socrates" 1. Note also *Untimely Meditations, Richard Wagner in Bayreuth* 4: "The individual must be dedicated to something transpersonal—that is the meaning of tragedy."

7. See pp. 14, 98, 99, and 103 for an important alternative view.

Chapter Two

Philosophy

"In knowledge, too, I feel only my will's joy in
begetting and becoming; and if there is innocence
in my knowledge, it is because the will to beget is in
it. Away from God and gods this will has lured me;
what could one create if gods—were there?!"

—*Thus Spoke Zarathustra II*,
"Upon the Blessed Isles"

Our prolonged beholding, our concentrated study of *Beyond Good
and Evil* draw vigor and justification not from the great beauty of the
work alone, but preeminently from our understanding that *BGE* is
the deepest and most comprehensive commentary on *Thus Spoke
Zarathustra*. Nietzsche regards his *Zarathustra* as the most profound
book the human race possesses, and Zarathustra himself as the high
point of humanity.[1] *BGE*, with its guiding theme of nobility, can be
called a restatement in more prosaic and accessible form of that
"most profound" *Zarathustra*.[2] One who fully appreciates *BGE* thus
stands at the second highest rung of the ladder into Nietzsche's soul. If we fall short of the last step up by a great distance,
Nietzsche's condemnation or disdain may include some solace: the
highest rung is reachable by none but himself. "My *Zarathustra* . . .
is an unintelligible book, because it is based on experiences I share
with nobody."[3]

11

AN IMMENSE DISPROPORTION

If the peaks of Nietzsche's thought must remain beyond our grasp, it is nevertheless possible through study of *BGE* to shed a few rays of light on them.[4] Indeed, as we have already seen, *BGE* promises a project of fantastic scope, a complete transformation of humanity and humanity's world. As he introduces it, Nietzsche in his prelude to a philosophy of the future appears to be no less ambitious than in the *Zarathustra* itself. Yet in *Ecce Homo*, Nietzsche's own brief commentary on *BGE* indicates an immense disproportion between *BGE* and *Zarathustra*. The *Zarathustra* is like the six-day creation by the almighty God of Genesis, and *BGE* is analogous to God's subsequent day of rest.[5] This disproportion is paralleled by an apparent lack of symmetry between the promise of the preface of *BGE* and the "reality" of the text.[6] Whereas the preface intimates that Nietzsche will commence an overturning of human thought from Plato down to himself, in fact Nietzsche devotes most of his time to an attack on modernity and seems unwilling to pursue any sustained attack on the premoderns. Nietzsche seems paradoxical here. How can the seventh day, the day of rest, be like a restatement of the six days of creation, how can a critique of modernity be equivalent to a critique of all previous philosophy, how can vehement negation be an expression of overwhelming affirmation?[7] We can put the formal solution to this riddle simply, even though the complete details comprise a monstrous and perplexing tangle. When Nietzsche criticizes modernity, ultimately his true enemy is classical antiquity; when he assaults the synthetic a priori, the ego, and the freedom of the will, he aims at their forefather, Plato. Moreover, the critique of philosophy altogether is not self-contained but rather prepares the way for an alternative to all previous philosophies, for the superman, for a noble philosophy of the future. *BGE* is indeed Nietzsche's "No-saying, No-doing" book, but its most critical aspect is its presentation of "a noble, Yes-saying type," i.e., its Yes-saying aspect.[8] One cannot begin to understand *BGE* either internally or in relation to *Zarathustra* unless one sees its major task as the replacement of Platonism by Nietzschean nobility. [9]

Plato is certainly the antagonist when Nietzsche attempts to establish his theoretical perspective. As already noticed, the first three chapters of *BGE* treat primarily theoretical matters, whereas the last five chapters, following a sort of interlude, concern practical matters. The order of *BGE* will determine the order of our study. So our first lengthy investigation will consider the theoretical perspective of Nietzsche contra Plato-Socrates. Concerning Plato-Socrates a brief caveat may be appropriate from the outset. For all the harsh ignominy that Nietzsche heaps upon the "naive" Plato and the "ugly, plebian" Socrates, Nietzsche does hold great admiration for both Plato and Socrates. Socrates, Nietzsche admits, "stands so near to me that I almost always fight a battle with him."[10] And Nietzsche calls Plato "the most beautiful growth of antiquity" and the provoker of the most "magnificent tension of the spirit" ever to exist on earth before Nietzsche.[11] These tributes take away nothing from Nietzsche's judgment of Plato-Socrates as the promulgator(s) of the very worst, most nightmarish human error; for one cannot hate those whom one does not first respect.[12] We speak of "Plato-Socrates," incidentally, not only because we know what we know of Socrates primarily through Plato and what we know of Plato primarily through Socratic dialogues in which Plato does not appear. Of greater weight, Nietzsche in his later writings generally tends to convict the Siamese pair of the crime of founding and spreading nihilism. The important distinctions between the two philosophers do not begin to match the gravity of what they have in common.

THEORY AND PRACTICE

We have vaguely identified the first major division of *BGE* as theoretical, but we must establish more precisely the link among the first three chapters, "On the Prejudices of Philosophers," "The Free Spirit," and "The Religious Matter."[13] Chapters 1 and 2 are propaedeutic to chapter 3, i.e., the overcoming of philosophies that hitherto never escaped the grip of Socratic Platonism is the precondition to a philosophy of the future that will subscribe to a new religious faith. The culmination of this faith will be "atheistic," but faithful nonetheless. The principal subject of the first major division, then, is the transformation of philosophy into Nietzschean religion. Chapter 1 attacks the past and especially Plato's dominion over the past; chapter 2 serves as a continuation, from the standpoint of the present, of chapter 1 and as a prolegomenon to chapter 3; and chapter 3 sanctifies the future with the culmination of the doctrine of the will to power, the eternal return. Chapter 1 introduces the doctrine of the will to power, chapter 2 develops it, and chapter 3 brings it to a peak. Under this interpretation the apex of Nietzsche's "metaphysics" is a willful affirmation or faith rather than a truth, a religion rather than a philosophy as traditionally understood. Since he finds at the bottom of all previous philosophies "the faith in the opposition of values," however, Nietzsche views his transformation of philosophy as the supplanting of one faith by another. "Perhaps the day will come when the most solemn concepts . . . will seem no more important to us than a child's toy and a child's pain seem to an old man—and perhaps 'the old man' will then be in need of another toy and another pain—still child enough, an eternal child!" (*BGE* 57, p. 259, which immediately follows the paragraph presenting the eternal return.)

Chapter 4 of *BGE*, the most mysterious chapter in a book otherwise hard to fathom, is entitled "Sayings and Interludes." Considering that this chapter comes immediately after the theoretical division and just before the practical division of the work, one might expect the content to provide the substantive link between theory and practice. And "interludes" is part of the title. We recall that when Plato's Socrates needed to supply the link between theory and practice, he devised a mathematical formula so complicated as to be for all practical purposes impenetrable. In that respect the plan of "Sayings and Interludes" does remind us of the nuptial number of Plato's *Republic*. There is a discernible subject matter of the whole, namely human psychology, and there are various ligatures here and there; but if a pattern of the whole ought to emerge from lengthy perusal of Chapter 4, that pattern escapes us, notwithstanding the accessibility of coherent schemes in the other chapters. We cannot speak with full confidence, but perhaps there is no strictly logical derivative from theory to practice. In the case of *BGE* that nullity would mean no rigorously logical line from the doctrine of the will to power to rule by Nietzsche's new nobility. If Nietzsche's teaching on nobility does not follow with logical necessity from the doctrine of the will to power, Nietzsche was in principle free to choose from any number of moralities to coincide with that doctrine. The will to power may prove to be a psychologically suggestive, but rationally insufficient, precondition for nobility. From this perspective the theoretical division serves indeed as a handmaiden, but as an inadequate handmaiden, to the moral division.

BEYOND VULGARIZED PLATONISM

The title of *Beyond Good and Evil: Prelude to a Philosophy of the Future* places Nietzsche at the point of transition between the morality of good and evil, i.e., slave morality—of which the most notable example is Christian morality—and a philosophy of the future.[14] Merely standing beyond the morality of Christianity can hardly be celebrated as a novelty, for did not all the ancients effortlessly avoid the trap of Christianity by dint of chronology alone? Nietzsche tacitly answers in the preface by remarking that Christianity is a vulgar manifestation of Platonism, of ugly, plebeian, Socratic Platonism. Socrates's conquest of Plato's nobility constitutes a victory by the plebs over their masters, so that under the influence of Socrates Plato plants the metaphysical seeds of slave morality.[15] Nietzsche would shock most of his contemporaries less and yet in important respects speak more accurately by entitling the book *Beyond Plato: Prelude to a Philosophy of the Future*.

The preface we have already addressed, but we should attend to Nietzsche's remark therein that his task is "wakefulness itself."[16] According to Nietzsche, human beings prior to himself are asleep, presumably meaning that their overall powers of reasoning and perception remain much weaker than they could be. Thus they take fictions for realities and fail to recognize what is genuinely real. We note that during sleep one does experience the same or similar passions as those during wakefulness, so "we whose task is wakefulness itself" would appear to have an intellectual rather than a moral objection against Plato and his followers: one could say that Nietzsche bests Plato simply in discerning the truth, although of course "the truth" might have moral consequences. Alternatively, one could call wakefulness itself the more complete expression of a passion that cannot come to full flower when a human being is asleep. Then Nietzsche's complaint against Plato might have primarily a moral thrust. In either case the question has already arisen whether wakefulness is indeed better than sleep. Nietzsche never leaves the question behind in *BGE*, and in consideration of its difficulty he sometimes seems to waver like a man desperately struggling to balance on a rope. This question of wakefulness—which is to say, this question of the will to truth and its origins and value—is the supreme question of *BGE*.

Nietzsche begins the text proper by making his supreme question explicit (*BGE* 1, p. 199), but his forthrightness in pursuing the question and setting forth his insights on it is not accompanied by a willingness to expound the necessary arguments. Nietzsche like the ancient Greek aristocracy considers it ignoble to present one's reasons: "honest men do not carry their reasons in their hands. . . . It is indecent to show all five fingers. What must first be proved is worth little. Wherever authority still forms part of good bearing . . . the dialectician is a kind of buffoon."[17] In this vein Nietzsche's way of proceeding presupposes that human rationality is a low thing: "The disgust with dirt can be so great that it keeps us from cleaning ourselves—from justifying ourselves" (*BGE* 119, p. 276). It is apparently left to the reader to devise the omitted justifications of Nietzsche's assertions as well as of Nietzsche's method. Is Nietzsche's procedure justified? Does he legitimately present insights and elaborations of insights while providing no arguments or at best only refutations of some alternatives? At this stage of our study we can only speak conditionally. First, omitting arguments would be theoretically justifiable if pristine rationality in argumentation were impossible.[18] Second, such omission would be philosophically defensible if tremendous insights would have to be sacrificed in order to devote time to proofs that in any event scholarly drudges can be depended upon to produce.[19] Third, arguments might be left unstated on sound moral grounds if their exposition would prove unsalutary to human life.[20]

Although Nietzsche speaks of self justification, especially public self-justification, as degrading, he in fact offers each of the foregoing three possible justifications of his method in print.[21] We must revise our description of his method accordingly: Nietzsche does not always rely entirely on his readers to construct his arguments, but when he does provide them he employs hints, asides, mysterious apothegms. Thus in his very method of expounding his view of truth, there can appear to be a wavering between traditional philosophizing and some kind of antiphilosophical reflection. One might say that Nietzsche both embraces and spurns dialectical reasoning.[22]

SOURCE OF THE WILL TO TRUTH

The first paragraph of *BGE* concerns, as mentioned, the will to truth (p. 199). The paragraph divides into two parts, corresponding to the two questions Nietzsche asks regarding the will to truth: whence does that will come and what is its value? As for the source of the will, his remarks in paragraphs 3 and 6 identify, as it were, the drives and instincts as the origin of all desire for truth (pp. 201, 203–04). But this identification is vague, so Nietzsche proceeds in paragraph 9 to define philosophy as "the most spiritual will to power" (p. 206). The meaning of the will to power is not immediately transparent, but one of the most revealing remarks about it in Nietzsche's writings occurs here in paragraph 9: the will to power is the drive "to 'the creation of the world,' to the causa prima" (ibid.). The will to power as presented in this passage is the will not only to be (i.e., to will) and to continue to be (to will) but also to indulge in the greatest imaginable self-expression and thus partake of the greatest imaginable power over everything in the world. The will to power is the will to be cause of all things, to be God almighty. The will to truth of philosophers, according to Nietzsche's novel doctrine, is simply a form of this will to power.

Elsewhere, Nietzsche gives a seemingly different version of the origin of the will to truth, an account he expresses in far more traditional terms. "Is it not the instinct of fear that bids us to know? Is the jubilation of those who attain knowledge not jubilation over the restoration of a false sense of security?"[23] This at-first-glance variant explanation of the will to truth turns out on reflection to be altogether compatible with the doctrine of the will to power, provided that one make one critical assumption. For why does one wish not only to be and to continue to be, but to indulge in the fullest imaginable self-expression, to put one's own stamp on everything in the world? Why does one wish to be omnipotent, to be God? Is it not because anything over which one lacks perfect control is unreliable and hence threatening? That is, in human beings is not the "instinct of fear" prior even to the will to power?[24] Perhaps Nietzsche has a single very probing answer to the question of *"what* in us really wants truth?"[25]

Nietzsche thus specifies only one of the two possible sources of the will to truth, namely fear of the unknown. The second possibility is that human reason inherently moves toward truth as the rock-bottom fulfillment of reason, that man qua rational desires to know simply because knowledge gratifies his appetitive reason, regardless of whether knowledge or ignorance more intensely arouses the passion of fear. The classical ancients gave prominence to this latter explanation in their writings, even as they took note of the former. This fact could suggest to some readers that the ancients employed the second account as a salutary varnish to cover the truer teaching. However, denial of the irreducibility of the pleasure of knowing cannot be taken as authoritative without a convincing demonstration. Nietzsche in *BGE* apparently fails even to construct a serious case for the disparaged "knowledge for its own sake," (Aristotle, *Metaphysics* 982A14–16), i.e., fails to do his dialectical duty, despite his glorification of the "more laudable truthfulness in every little question mark that [a philosopher] places after [his] special words and favorite doctrines . . . than in all [his] solemn gestures and trumps before accusers and law courts" (*BGE* 25, p. 266).[26] Nietzsche does address "knowledge for its own sake" in so many words, but he brushes it off half-flippantly as "the last snare of morality" and sweepingly asserts without argument that "[t]he attraction of knowledge would be small if one did not have to overcome so much shame on the way" (*BGE* 64 and 65, p. 269).

One might characterize Nietzsche's lover of truth as overwhelmed by childlike fear of the dark. If the will to truth does truly derive from fear of the unknown, one can dismiss the philosophic way of life as neurotic and tell the philosopher to grow up, get a grip on himself, admit the folly of his childish fears, and cease to tremble at the darkness. The lover of truth as described by Nietzsche may not even retort that fear of the unknown belongs to his nature, for one might then accuse him of having a distinctively defective nature; most people, after all, control their fear of the dark enough to roll over and go to sleep. For that matter, the question remains open whether and to what extent one's nature can be overcome.

VALUE OF THE WILL TO TRUTH

The first paragraph of *BGE* has (to repeat) two parts, the one we have just discussed on the origin of the will to truth, and one that asks, what is the value of that will? Nietzsche does not make explicit the relation between the two questions, but in light of the foregoing considerations a very tight connection comes to view. The question of the origin of the will to truth leads necessarily to the question of its value; for if the will to truth comes into being out of something deeper, such as human fear, it seems that will will not, or at least ought not, to continue to pursue truth when truth begins to cause deeper harm than gratification or other benefit for the fearful human being. This thought is the principal suggestion of the first paragraph.[27] To pursue devastatingly horrible truths would seem contradictory for a will to truth that emerges out of fearfulness. And yet such contradiction does occur in man, as the case of the noble Oedipus demonstrates. Oedipus tenaciously pursued certain truths until the horror of their eventual discovery provoked him to dash out his eyes. Surely it can be asked in Oedipus's case, "Why not rather untruth? And uncertainty? Even ignorance?" Immediately after making that inquiry, Nietzsche does introduce Oedipus, and in such a way as to make the Oedipus problem as severe as it can possibly be, for Nietzsche identifies himself with Oedipus. Once can perhaps begin to explain the aberrant will to truth in Oedipus in terms of his anticipation of useful rather than pernicious truths at the end of his search. "When one has finished building one's house, one suddenly realizes that in the process one has learned something that one really needed to know in the worst way—before one began" (*BGE* 277, p. 413). Had Oedipus only known that the truths he seeks are destructive, he might have desisted from his search for truth and remained a king. According to Nietzsche, what Oedipus needed to know from the beginning, Sophocles teaches his readers in the moral of *Oedipus the King* and *Oedipus at Colonus*: "The edge of wisdom turns against the wise: wisdom is a crime against nature."[28] Nietzsche's Sophocles in *Oedipus at Colonus* substitutes for Silenus as the example par excellence of wisdom. Nietzsche bursts out with Silenus's potentially unnerving wisdom in a remarkably eloquent passage in *The Birth of Tragedy*:

There is an ancient story that King Midas hunted in the forest a long time for the wise Silenus, the companion of Dionysus, without capturing him. When Silenus at last fell into his hands the king asked him what is the best and most desirable of all things for man. Fixed and immovable, the demigod said not a word, until at last, urged by the king, he gave a shrill laugh and broke out into these words: "Oh wretched, ephemeral race, children of chance and misery, why do you compel me to tell you what it would be most expedient for you not to hear? What is best of all is utterly beyond your reach: not to be born, not to be, to be nothing. But the second best for you is— to die soon."[29]

The truth behind the Oedipus story could not be uglier. Yet Nietzsche celebrates rather than condemns the real knower of that truth, Sophocles the artist. What can unriddle this paradox? Perhaps Silenus's wisdom, though somehow profound, is not entirely comprehensive. If any "comprehensive" wisdom can be achieved, transforming the darkest pessimism into the most glowing affirmation, Nietzsche's Zarathustra presumably attains it. If, however, Nietzsche does waver on the question of the will to truth, he also remains uncertain whether Silenus's wisdom is not indeed the final wisdom—Silenus is after all the companion of Dionysus—i.e., Nietzsche also suffers from a fundamental ambivalence over whether life is worth living.

After introducing Oedipus, Nietzsche makes a qualified claim of originality. "And though it scarcely seems credible, it finally almost seems to us as if the problem [of the value of truth] has never even been put so far—as if we were the first to see it, fix it with our eyes, and *risk* it. For it does involve a risk, and perhaps there is none that is greater" (*BGE* 1, p. 199). One should not overlook the importance of the qualifier "almost": Sophocles, at least, must have seen the problem of the value of truth.[30] Our principal question here, though, is why Nietzsche claims that such a great risk, perhaps the greatest, attaches to his questioning of the value of truth. He does not identify that risk here. Perhaps it is the risk of losing truth forever, and therewith of losing the possibility of an intelligible world. Why, then, take such a risk? One conceivable, and maybe the only tenable justification for the gamble, is that living with truth could be more miserable than living without it.

FAITH IN THE OPPOSITION OF VALUES

Nietzsche turns in the second paragraph to what he calls faith in the opposition of values. The paragraph consists of two parts, a statement in quotation marks by an unnamed metaphysician who believes in the opposition of values, and Nietzsche's expression of doubt, set forth in his own name, of this fundamental faith of the metaphysicians. The unidentified speaker doubts that anything could originate from its opposite, especially not truth out of error, or the will to truth out of the will to deception. The things of the highest value, according to the anonymous metaphysician, cannot have their source in "this transitory, seductive, deceptive, paltry world," i.e., in the world of the senses; the things of the highest value derive from the bosom of Being, from the realm of the eternal, of the hidden God or the thing-in-itself (*BGE* 2, p. 200). Thus Plato's overcoming of the motley world of the senses (*BGE* 14, p. 212) is at the bottom of "all" metaphysics before Nietzsche: the world of the noumena is good, the world of the phenomena is bad. The philosopher into whose mouth the full quotation might most appropriately be placed is not Plato-Socrates or Aristotle, but Kant. Nietzsche's intention appears to be to assimilate Kant, as well as Christianity, to the religion[31] of Plato and Aristotle, but in fact he merely reminds us of how markedly their teachings vary from Kant's. Where, for example, does Aristotle flatly deny that selfless deeds originate out of selfishness? Might not *phronesis*, the proper ruler of the moral virtues, be fundamentally selfish?[32] As for Plato, to begin with he never speaks in his own name except in the titles of the dialogues and in his letters. When Plato's Socrates does address the origin of philosophy, notably in the palinode of the *Phaedrus*, he speaks under proclaimed duress and in the form of myths. And Socrates's language and imagery in the palinode are not only not unusually abstract, but on the contrary especially varied, concrete, and sensual. Furthermore, the noetic pilot of the soul as Socrates characterizes it evidently cannot set the soul into motion, and the erotic part of the soul, which seems at least primarily responsible for the motion of the soul, is quite ugly. Socrates does speak of "colorless and shapeless and intangible beingness (*ousia*) being in fact (*ontos ousa*)," but he does so only after the episode of veiling himself that recalls his death at the end of the *Phaedo*: perhaps Plato is suggesting that no man actually encounters the intangible world unless he has come back from the dead, that belief in any world but the world of the senses is altogether nonsensical.[33] At any rate it is far from clear that the writings of the ancients testify convincingly to the naivete Nietzsche imputes to them.

Nietzsche treats the metaphysicians' fundamental faith in the opposition of values as a mere prejudice, never before questioned by anyone. He strongly suggests, without asserting in his own name, that the true, the truthful, and the selfless are so inextricably bound up with deception, selfishness, and lust that they have the same essence (*wesensgleich zu sein*). To the extent that distinctions can still be made, "wicked" things such as deception, selfishness, and lust may be more valuable for life than "good" things. Thus in the second paragraph Nietzsche gives tentative answers to the two questions of the first: the will to truth originates not out of itself alone but out of something deeper that cannot be separated from the will to deception; and the value of the will to truth is perhaps lower for life than the value of the will to deception. These answers are emphatically hypothetical and yet so radical that their treatment requires a new species (*Gattung*) of philosophers. "Speaking in all seriousness," Nietzsche professes to see such new philosophers coming up. The seriousness of his discourse in anticipating the advent of such philosophers of the future derives from his intention singlehandedly to bring them into being. The first two paragraphs can now be summarized as follows: Nietzsche begins by questioning the will to truth in order to cast aspersions on the will to truth, at least in part in order to bring about a new race of philosophers, subject to and yet suspicious of the will to truth. From the beginning Nietzsche's philosophizing serves an educational project, the creation of human beings in his own image. Whether the fufillment of such a project would represent the overcoming of prejudice depends on whether arguments against the belief in opposite values are cogent and, if so, on whether the distinction between prejudiced and unprejudiced thought can survive the extirpation of that belief.

THE DOMINION OF INSTINCT OVER THOUGHT

In the third paragraph, Nietzsche in a most authoritative fashion— "I say to myself"—includes philosophical thinking among instinctive activities and thus openly erodes the boundary line between prejudiced and unprejudiced thought. Apparently his educational project does not aim at rooting out prejudice per se. Consciousness, as Nietzsche describes it, is simply the unfolding of the instincts into the realm of thought, such that the instincts secretly guide philosophical thinking. The impression that logic proceeds according to its own rules is deceptive, for the rules of logic are set by the rules of the body for preserving a certain type of life. Thus men bow to the rule of noncontradiction not because of its inherent validity but because genuflecting to the authority of the rule contributes to their strength. Prior to Nietzsche, the ground of the logical rule always escaped conscious scrutiny, so men cannot be said to have calculated the advantages of the rule of contradiction before adopting it. But in a manner of speaking the body does "calculate" the overall advantages, although the body is too stupid to do anything but dispose the consciousness to a general receptivity to the rule of contradiction. In revolting against the mandate of the body by doubting the universal validity of the rules of logic, Nietzsche lays claim to philosophical novelty. This claim would seem justified if he means that hereafter men ought consciously to choose the false over the true whenever the false conduces to human life.

The fourth paragraph begins as follows:

> The falseness of a judgment is for us not necessarily an objection to a judgment; in this respect our new language may sound strangest. The question is to what extent it is life-promoting, life-preserving, species-preserving, perhaps even species-cultivating. And we are fundamentally inclined to claim that the falsest judgments (which include the synthetic judgments a priori) are the most indispensable for us . . . [pp. 201–2].

In this same paragraph Nietzsche boldly dubs the rules of logic "fictions," asserts that the unconditional and self-identical is a mere invention, and calls mathematical explanation of the world "falsification," although of course all these falsehoods have utility for life. Nietzsche's judgment that logic, mathematics, and metaphysics generally are infected with untruths designed to anthropomorphize the world implies that Nietzsche has seen the truth of the nonanthropomorphized world against which he judges fictions. Nietzsche, not some pre-Socratic like Democritus or early modern such as Spinoza, is the first truly to see this world in which man is not the only measure of things (*BGE* 3, p. 201).

As Nietzsche well knows, his position in paragraphs 3 and 4 invites objection. For example, if philosophical thinking is inevitably

instinctive, is it not impossible to achieve a standpoint from which
the deanthropomorphized world comes to view? Actually he has
not yet ruled out such a standpoint, for he asserts not that all conscious thinking without exception is an instinctive activity, but that
"the greater part" is instinctual and that "most" of a philosopher's
conscious thought is (*BGE* 3). Nietzsche thus seems to allow for
the possibility of a non-Hegelian sort of absolute moment. Such an
absolute moment appears necessary in order to sort acceptable
truths from those to be rejected according to their value for life. For
how can one achieve a solid grasp of what is valuable for life without a full understanding of what is useless or baneful? In the decisive respect, then, must one not attain reliable knowledge of the
whole truth?

One can also ask what sense it makes to call the principle of noncontradiction an instrument for preserving a certain type of life, unless that type be human or rational life. And is not rational life precisely life dominated or heavily influenced by the principle of
noncontradiction? Does the principle turn out to be a device for preserving *itself*? This line of questioning presupposes Aristole's observation that man is the rational animal. We see that the human
species is by nature superior to the other animals; what is distinctively human, namely the rational faculty, must provide the ground
of that superiority; and the development of this faculty constitutes
man's peculiar virtue. Nietzsche violently objects to this paradigm.
In his view man transcends the other animals, if at all, because his
will to power is more spiritual, or in more Aristotelian language, because man has loftier passions. Aristotle would reply that man's
greater "spirituality" or higher passions derive exactly from his rationality. What distinguishes the higher passions from the lower
ones if not the pervasiveness of reason in the higher? Nietzsche
could perhaps rejoin that rationality may be a precondition for the
higher affects by analogy as ingestion of victuals is a precondition
for thinking, but creative self-expression is far superior to mere ra-
tiocination.[34] Aristotle in turn would probably complain that creativity per se is meaningless, that every example of "creativity"
must amount to either a prudential act proceeding from rational de-
liberation or else an instance of childish folly. Nietzsche might retort that this Aristotelian argument on behalf of reason presupposes
already the authority of the principle of noncontradiction and the

supremacy of reason. Whereupon Aristotle would likely exclaim that all sane human thought presupposes the principle of noncontradiction. What basis, Aristotle might ask, exists for preferring your understanding, what basis that does not rely on the rules of reason? What basis, other than *naked preference*? At this point one can imagine Nietzsche's singing songs and pointing upwards in the direction of the noble Zarathustra. But one can legitimately ask Aristotle what basis there is for preferring his understanding, what basis that neither assumes blind faith in the authority of reason nor appeals to the utility of the principles of reason for life?

Nietzsche also insists, as we have seen, that mathematics is a system of lies under the dominion of the instincts. He does not elaborate, but it is clear enough that mathematicizing the world both serves the practical sciences and fosters the delusion, in his view, of theoretical understanding. He might further point out that mathematics begins with definitions laid down by acts of the human will. These definitions refer to "givens" that are not strictly to be found in the realm of experience. Is it not clear that the "truths" of mathematics are actually fictions?

The issue requires further reflection. We can agree that a mathematical definition says *what* a thing is and not *that* it is. But does experience play no role at all when we distinguish between the real and imaginary number systems?[35] What does it mean that even some birds clearly distinguish between, and count with their cries, one, two, and three intruders? Is not the applicability of mathematics for the sciences a possible indication that lines and circles might have some ontic status in our world of experience, a status independent of human creation? And is it not inconclusive that the circles we actually see are imperfect? Indeed, is it not true that *to the unaided eye* some circles we see are perfect? Nietzsche reminds us of *The Critique of Pure Reason*, where Kant shows that we do not really see a circle that exists outside of us; rather, we come into contact with billions of multifarious pulsations from a mysterious manifold that activates our innate propensity for conjuring images of circles. Yet do not the different images we conjure depend upon the different natures of the various pulsations with which we come into contact? Must there not be in the so-called manifold different sequences of various patterns of pulsations—and if there are patterns, why not circles? Admittedly, if as Kant contends "quantity" should prove to be merely a category of the understanding, mathematics would subsist in the rational mind alone and not in the world. Still, how can we *know* that quantity derives strictly from the structure of the mind rather than from the world with which the mind is in contact? Perhaps Nietzsche would answer that mathematics deals with relations that necessarily depend upon a *relator*, or that the concept of quantity presupposes identity and difference in classes or forms that do not exist by nature.

PROBITY

Nietzsche's "recognition" that untruths are preconditions of life places him beyond good and evil; in the most notable morality of good and evil, Jesus is the way, the truth, and the light, and the highest fulfillment of life can be had only through the truth of Christ. As already indicated, however, the ultimate culprit behind the crime of spreading the morality of good and evil is Plato. According to Plato's *Republic*, political life depends on conventions that will perish in the light of pristine truth. Every city must be built on lies, in the best case on noble lies. To this extent, then, Plato and Nietzsche concur. Nietzsche can get "beyond" Plato only at a suprapolitical level—even the philosopher must lie to himself, even he would perish from direct exposure to the truth.[36]

The fifth paragraph concerns the probity of philosophers. Nietzsche's suspicion and mockery of all philosophers—here he does not say all philosophers so far—is directed not at their innocence (*Unschuld*),[37] but at their deficient probity (*Redlichkeit*). Nietzsche assails the philosophers for pretending to arrive at their "truths" through an unprejudiced dialectic, when in fact their "truths" are first inspirational hunches shaped by the wish of the heart and only thereafter "conclusions" of "pure dialectical reasoning." Quite likely the philosophers cannot help being advocates. But they could, if they wished, admit their prejudices openly. Thus philosophers lack a moral virtue that Nietzsche implies he possesses, "the courage of the conscience"[38] to acknowledge the prejudiced character of his "truths" and thus even to mock them. Nietzsche will indulge his probity, i.e., his will to truth, in playful criticism of himself, whereas his attack on previous philosophers for the sake of philosophers of the future will be entirely serious (*BGE* 2 and preface). Unlike the metaphysicians, Nietzsche is strong enough to face cheerfully the truth that there is no truth. Why, then, is he so sober in his moral project? Does his moral project depend upon the recognition of a truth that cannot be faced cheerfully?[39] If so, it would not be amazing that Nietzsche should embrace exuberantly the "truth" that there is no truth, for that "truth" would be useful to life and thus meet his sovereign criterion. Of course in that case Nietzsche himself would ultimately be lacking in probity, just as his predecessors were. Thus all philosophers, not just all so far, would lack probity.

HEALTH

At the end of paragraph 5, Nietzsche's psychological account of Spinoza's philosophy deserves attention. According to Nietzsche, the geometrical method is intended to intimidate Spinoza's readers and thereby guard against anyone's attacking (*angreifen*) Spinoza's vulnerability (*Angreifbarkeit*). Spinoza in the *Ethics* attempts to disguise his inner sickness. Just as without the Palladium Troy could not survive, so does Spinoza's survival depend upon his masquerade as a spokesman of the apodictic. In connection with Spinoza's alleged sickness Nietzsche calls him a hermit, a remark that might seem gratuitous unless we recall that Nietzsche himself is a famous hermit who makes much of his being one. Perhaps he invites us to wonder about other similarities. Specifically, might Nietzsche, too, engage in a masquerade of existential significance? For the time being we abandon that inquiry as too tenuous and speculative. At all events, Spinoza cannot be judged sick except against some standard of health. Spiritual or mental health can perhaps best be described as the disposition or capacity to fulfill one's deepest fulfillable desires and to accept with equanimity the unfulfillable nature of other deep desires. If sickness differs from health, as Nietzsche indicates, some human actions must be judged untailored to the fulfillment of the actor's deepest desires. Ergo, if we want to know what a human being's deepest desires are, we cannot rely on that person's actions to give us the answer. A man may repeatedly strike his head against a brick wall not out of the wish for a cerebral concussion but out of confusion about what he truly wants. How, then, can we discover what a human being's deepest desires truly are? Aristotle, beholding man as the rational animal and portraying fully developed reason as the peak of human virtue, identifies the longing to attain wisdom as the deepest desire because that aspiration so profoundly accords with human nature. Dismissing Aristotle as superficial, Nietzsche asserts that the most fundamental desire is the most active desire, the will to power, the will willing the will to itself. "At last one loves one's desire (*Begierde*) and not what is desired (*das Begehrte*)" (*BGE* 175, p. 283). At first glance the universality of the will to power could appear to dissolve the distinction between healthy and unhealthy desires. On the contrary, though, we can now clearly see that dichotomy as a difference of degree rather than of kind, for health equals strength of the will, and sickness, weakness of the will. Here, too, Nietzsche liberates us from the faith in the opposition of values. In particular the philosopher's health depends on the spirituality, the sublime strength, of his will to power. A lack of probity, such as Spinoza's, signifies a weak will. Thus Nietzsche's understanding of health stands or falls on the soundness of his explanation of the will to truth as an outgrowth of the will to power.

CONVICTION

Nietzsche appears merely to develop further his critique of the prejudices of the metaphysicians in paragraph 6, where he contends that alpha and omega for every philosophy is the philosopher's moral intention. This intention expresses the order of rank of the demonic drives that comprise his self or soul. Nothing whatever in the philosopher is impersonal, least of all his morality and thus his philosophy. At first Nietzsche seems to exempt himself from this characterization, for he speaks in the past tense of philosophers "so far," but by the end of the paragraph he speaks of "the philosopher" and uses the present tense. Nietzsche's probity may require his tacit acknowledgement of the devilish, idiosyncratic, and hence dubious character of his own morality, but his seriousness about his morality makes him reluctant to do so explicitly. Like Spinoza, Nietzsche needs a mask in order to inscribe his teachings into the hearts of humanity (cf. preface, pp. 192–93). If, however, his morality is indeed supreme in his own philosophy, why leave room for doubt about that morality at all? Why expose himself to the grave objection that his imperative, too, means at bottom "live according to life," and to the boomeranging question "Why make a principle of what you yoursel[f] are and must be?" (*BGE* 9, p. 205)? A discord dominates the relationship between his morality and his probity, and despite his musical talent, he seems never completely to transcend the disharmony. In other words, when Nietzsche attempts to subordinate his will to truth completely to his will to power, he fails.[40]

After asserting that every philosophy is subservient to an individual drive in the philosopher, Nietzsche applies his generalization to a particular case by psychoanalyzing Epicurus. By an odd coincidence, Nietzsche happens to choose as his patient a philosopher who, like Nietzsche, openly denies the otherworldly, affirms the body, and takes on Plato as his supreme enemy. "Epicurus" charges Plato and the Platonists with being actors in whom there is nothing genuine (*BGE* 7, p. 204), and his entire corpus is written out of rage and ambition against Plato. Thus Epicurus's whole doctrine stems from his irrational drives, and this most important fact about him was not noticed when the Greeks posthumously "discovered" him. Nietzsche truly discovers him for the first time here in *BGE*. In what respect the maligned Plato is an actor, however, Nietzsche-Epicurus does not reveal. Perhaps Plato's acting consists in pretending to philosophize impersonally, to think from the standpoint of the pure spirit. That is, Plato is not genuine because, like the other philosophers, Plato is deficient in the virtue of probity. It seems fair to say that Epicurus, too, is disingenuous, for his own pretense to be first of all a lover of truth fooled his readers and followers for at least a century and perhaps millennia; but Plato is more expert at acting and staging than Epicurus.

Hard on the heels of the exposure of the basic animus of Epicurus comes Nietzsche's remark that at a certain point every philosopher's "conviction" appears on the stage. Philosophers qua philosophers are men of the stage, it seems. Nietzsche likens the philosopher's conviction to a beautiful and most powerful or brave (*fortissimus*) ass. Every philosophy is guided by a stupidity, then, that is nevertheless a *beautiful* stupidity. Asses as such may be unsightly, but evidently an ass that is fortissimos must also be beautiful; compare the yes-saying ass of *Zarathustra* IV. Not having carved out any exception for himself, presumably Nietzsche, too, philosophizes under the

dominion of a stupid conviction that is nonetheless beautiful. Aston-
ishingly, Nietzsche seems to identify his own stupid conviction in
the following paragraph (*BGE* 9, p. 206), where he first speaks of the
doctrine of the will to power, his "fundamental teaching." How can
one remain subject to a stupid conviction that one proclaims to be
stupid? Nietzsche indicates he remains unperturbed by this question—if the doctrine of the will to power should prove to be merely
his own idiosyncrasy, so much the better (*BGE* 22, pp. 220–21)! He
has already explained why he might adhere to a stupid conviction:
the falseness of a judgment is not necessarily an objection to a judgment (*BGE* 4, p. 201). But he has also already supplied us with what
is necessarily an objection to a judgment, namely its failure to enhance life. Nietzsche can justify maintaining his conviction in the
doctrine of the will to power only if it proves to be a useful beast of
burden.

LIFE

We are not entitled to question the doctrine of the will to power in the
name of life unless we reflect on the essential tendency of life for
Nietzsche. His remark in the paragraph under consideration is not
sufficiently revealing: "Living—is that not precisely wanting to be
other than . . . nature? Is not living estimating, preferring, being unjust, being limited, wanting to be different?" Later in chapter 1 Nietzsche disdainfully dismisses the familiar answer of classical modernity
that the fundamental tendency of a living organism is to preserve itself (*BGE* 13, p. 211). As for Aristotle's famous formula equating life
with self-motion, Nietzsche deprecates the distinction between vol-
untary motion and involuntary motion as an obsolete simplicism that
depends on the absurd concept of a *causa sui* (*BGE* 21, pp. 218–19).
Life in Nietzsche's view is the tendency of the living thing to let out
its strength, i.e., its will to power. In the form of a persona Life tells
a bewildered Zarathustra who she is: "*I am what must always overcome itself* . . . [T]he truth was not hit by him who shot at it with the
word of the 'will to existence': that will does not exist! For, what does
not exist cannot will; but as for what is in existence, how could that
still want existence?! Only where there is life is there also will: not
will to life but—thus I teach you—will to power. There is much that

life esteems more highly than life itself; but out of the esteeming itself speaks the will to power."[41] The meaning of life is altogether indistinguishable from the doctrine of the will to power.

Insofar as the teaching about the will to power and the teaching
about the meaning of life are identical, it might seem fatuous to try
to judge the doctrine of the will to power before the bar of life.
Quite the opposite applies, for the possibility exists that the creative
self could suffer injury exactly as a result of the promulgation of the
true doctrine about its essential nature.[42] Nietzsche has made abun-
dantly clear that the truth need not be salutary.[43] He does promulgate
the doctrine of the will to power, so presumably he believes that it
increases the strength or reduces the vulnerability of the creative
self that longs to discharge its power.

Plato and Aristotle might well complain that Nietzsche's account
of the essence of life as will to power displays far more creativity
than understanding, more wishful thinking than practical wisdom.
According to the received dispensation of classical antiquity, the living thing that moves itself has a *fixed* essence. Precisely the un-
changing elements discernible in the flux make the world intelligible
and prudent human behavior possible. Only for the superficial can
these fixities serve as icons of any Socratic-Platonic-Aristotelian
piety, as the best readers of the *Parmenides*, the *Nicomachean Ethics*,
and the *Metaphysics* will readily grasp; rather, comprehension of
these fixities in their problematical character emerges from a self-
critical dialectic rich in irony and humor. Nietzsche, with his dia-
metrically opposed version of life as essentially self-overcoming or
flux, disparages as misguided and vengeful the ancient effort to impose stability on the world of becoming. In *Twilight of the Idols* Nietzsche calls Flaubert a nihilist because he prefers thinking at rest:
any failure to celebrate, even the least reservation against the world
of ubiquitous motion, is nihilism. "The sedentary life is the very sin
against the Holy Spirit."[44] Confronted with such comical exaggeration, we have to remain alert for other signs of irony — such as Nietzsche at times seems to overlook in the Socratics of antiquity. At any
rate Nietzsche knows there is no "Being" behind doing, effecting,
becoming. There is no lightning behind the flash in the sky, because
the lightning *is* the flash.[45] If life is creative self-overcoming, the motion of life is not even fixed by an end or set of ends, for a goal once
reached is automatically transcended. However, does the concept of

motion not require a series of specific stations through which the moving object passes? More seriously, Plato and Aristotle would accuse Nietzsche of failing to articulate what it is that does the moving from one point to another, i.e., what the self is that overcomes itself. Were Nietzsche to respond impatiently that the lightning is the flash, that nothing lies behind the discharge of energy, Aristotle would undoubtedly rejoin that such a discharge of energy occurs only in an atmosphere with a determinate, describable nature. Nietzsche's account of the basic meaning of life can, on the basis of such considerations as these, be regarded as an exacerbation rather than a correction of the difficulty of the classical modern assertion that life is fundamentally animated by the desire to preserve itself.[46] The self that desires to preserve itself—or for Nietzsche, to create and discharge itself—has not been illuminated. Nietzsche's awareness of this difficulty is suggested by his treatment of Life as personified in the *Zarathustra*. Both at the beginning and at the end of Life's discourse Nietzsche calls her unfathomable. At the end of his exchange with Life, when Zarathustra is told "now speak to me of your wisdom," Zarathustra is silent.[47] Nevertheless, he goes on to instruct those who are the wisest in the teaching of life.[48] Although Nietzsche rightly considers his teaching on life problematic and paradoxical, his view that life is "essentially" creativity would seem to be final.

By no accident, in the very paragraph in which the doctrine of the will to power is introduced, "nature" is first mentioned. The main point of the paragraph could be said to be that living "according to nature" amounts to nothing other than exercising one's will to power and calling such exercise "natural." In other words, Nietzsche in paragraph 9 assimilates nature to will. Such assimilation, we will see, comes to a peak in the fifth chapter of *BGE*, which the ninth paragraph anticipates. Nietzsche proceeds in this paragraph as follows: First he describes nature as Spinoza might have done, as being "extravagantly wasteful beyond measure, indifferent beyond measure, without purposes and consideration, without mercy and justice" (p. 205). Nietzsche correctly points out that living according to such an indifferent nature is impossible because human action requires choices that in turn require preferences or "values." Second, Nietzsche considers the possibility that nature means the way of a human being, human nature as irrepressible inner compulsion, and rightly observes that in this sense all men inevitably live according to nature, so extolling the virtues of so living is again absurd. Finally, Nietzsche treats nature as the matter of the world over which the Stoics and indeed all philosophers tyrannize (p. 206). The first view of nature is that of classical modernity, and the third view is Nietzsche's (cf. p. 61 below). The second view, evidently ascribed to the Stoics, is perhaps a caricature of antiquity, although it, too, bears a curious resemblance to Nietzsche's teaching on man. Teleological nature, nature in the sense of the standard according to which an acorn should grow into a magnificent oak, is implicitly dismissed by Nietzsche as mere human construction, no doubt because in reality nature more often than not pulverizes acorns, so magnificent oaks are but "unnatural" accidents. Nietzsche rejects the ancient view of teleological nature because he takes the modern view as his starting point. But is it not more sensible to describe an acorn in terms of a natural inner striving to become an oak than to represent it as a mere indifferent piece of matter? Nietzsche can be said to meet this complaint with his second notion of nature, in which he asks why what is ineluctably striven for should be extolled. This question might eventually be turned against his own teachings on nobility.[49] At any rate, the second view of nature corrects the indifference of the first nature without supplying a natural ground for what is high in life. The third nature, the will to power, is creativity itself, and can therefore create the ground for the high. *Unless*, that is, the natural matter for the will to power is not altogether formless but *resists* the will to power: for their clinging to the hope of tyrannizing over nature, Nietzsche calls the Stoics insane! The inclination, then, is to conclude that Nietzsche's assimilation of nature to the will to power remains incomplete, that the will to power is frustrated by that first nature which is antithetical to life.

PSYCHOANALYSIS

The tenth paragraph marks the break in parts of the first chapter of *BGE*. The first nine paragraphs complete the initial presentation of the doctrine of the will to power, and roughly speaking the remaining fourteen paragraphs apply that doctrine to particular philosophical and scientific teachings by attributing them to personality traits of their propounders. More precisely, in the second "half" of the chapter Nietzsche sometimes psychoanalyzes, sometimes makes genuine metaphysical counterarguments, sometimes mainly spoofs his victims, and thrice even adverts explicitly again to the will to power (*BGE* 13, 20, and 23, pp. 211, 220, and 221). There are ligatures between sections, but they are looser than those of the first part. Even under close analysis, Nietzsche conveys a greater light-heartedness—except in the three paragraphs that address the doctrine of the will to power by name. In the second part of the chapter he never refers to himself as speaking seriously. Apparently Nietzsche considers it necessary to provide comic relief in the wake of the profound seriousness of his introduction of the doctrine of the will to power. This comic relief comes at the expense of Christianity and modernity. Plato is mentioned by name only once, respectfully and almost amicably: the Platonic way of thought is called noble (*vornehm*, *BGE* 14, p. 212). One wonders whether the agon with Plato, *the* opponent of the doctrine of the will to power, is too serious to be made apparent in this lighter part of chapter 1. But the three very serious turns to that doctrine, especially at the chapter's end where he says psychology shall become queen of the sciences *once again* (*BGE* 23, p. 122), remind us that he has forgotten neither the will to power nor his enemy Plato. The ostensible assault on Christianity and modernity is fundamentally a roundabout assault on antiquity.

A. THE SPIRIT OF REVENGE

Nietzsche begins paragraph 10 with the clear intimation that what moves his European contemporaries to attack the problem of the actual world versus the apparent world is some psychic need other than the will to truth. He does not identify the passion, perhaps because such a discussion could become too serious, but rather changes the subject almost entirely (p. 206). Readers familiar with other Nietzschean writings will have no trouble guessing that the passion in question is the spirit of revenge. Philosophers prior to Nietzsche are the most noteworthy harborers of this spirit, and among them the most notable is Plato. The spirit of revenge is hatred of the world, i.e., the world of becoming, and concomitant love of (nonexistent) Being. Logos inherently serves this hatred of becoming by "imposing categories such as 'being' on man, but one can realize that the empirical world—the world known through the testimony of the senses—contradicts one's categories. Previous philosophers have reacted to this realization by slandering the empirical world, but Nietzsche, who is beyond the snares of language and reason because he recognizes them as snares, exposes all notions of a 'true world' as a slander on the empirical and only world."[50] Nietzsche presumes to know that the only real world is the world of becoming, because the senses, which do not lie, convey only impressions of becoming or rather of things in motion. Heraclitus was wrong to think that the senses convey impressions of both motion and rest, or rather of things both moving and resting, for the notion of rest is a mere construction.[51] The argument that "motion" makes no sense except in terms of rest will not be revived. Instead, we now ask whether Nietzsche's correction of Heraclitus, by restricting the content of sensations, goes far enough. When, for example, I reach out with my moistened hand and feel air particles rush into it, is it not my interpretation rather than sheer sensation that leads me to conclude that the air, or at any rate something outside my body, is moving? First this nerve cell is stimulated, then that one—why assume an external movement to be the cause? More radically, why presuppose any cause? (Cf. *BGE* 16 and 34.) At any rate, it may well be that neither rest nor motion external to my body can be conveyed by the senses alone.[52] Would we have to doubt the soundness of Nietzsche's rejection of rationalism in favor of the creative self or the will to power if belief in the "apparent world" of becoming should prove to have no more secure basis than does belief in the "true world"? Or would he try to take this line of attack, too, as a confirmation of his position?

B. SKEPTICS AND IDEALISTS

For the moment Nietzsche appears to leave these questions far in the background. Now he turns somewhat abruptly to two opposite types of soul, each of which is defective, but each of which suggests to Nietzsche a genuinely virtuous form of itself. The first type is the puritanical fanatic of conscience whose will to truth leads him "to prefer a secure nothing over an uncertain something," i.e., to prefer to rest secure with trivialities or, more likely, with knowledge of the worthlessness of life or knowledge of his own ignorance, rather than to affirm ultimately dubious values or "truths" however useful. Nietzsche calls this first soul despairing, dead tired, and nihilistic (p. 205). We are led to think of the Third Essay of *The Genealogy of Morals* in general and particularity of the Socrates of Nietzsche's *Twilight of the Idols*:[53] Nietzsche's modern skeptic inherits his soul from the estate of Socratic decadence. Accordingly, Nietzsche does praise the extravagant and adventurous brave-heartedness (*Mut*) of the first type of soul, even as he warns against its nihilism. Evidently the really virtuous version of the first soul-type would put its bravery or courage (*Tapferkeit*) into the service, rather than into the denial, of life.

The second soul-type discussed in paragraph 10 evinces mistrust of "the village-fair motleyness and patchiness" of modern ideas. This soul quite properly holds vigorous and cheerful life supreme in his economy, but his will to truth is defective, for he longs for ancient faiths to bolster him against modernity, e.g., for the immortal soul and the old God. Thus the second soul escapes the modern form of Socratic skepticism only by sinking into the pit of Platonic idealism. But the essential thing (*das Wesentliche*) about men of the second soul-type is not their desire to return to ancient faiths, but their repulsion by modernity. Had they only "somewhat *more* strength, flight, boldness, and artistry," says Nietzsche, "they would want to get out—and not back!" (p. 207)[54] The repellent morass of modernity is just an extension of the swamp of antiquity from which one can escape only by a daring act of philosophic innovation. Thus by their incomplete virtue both soul-types point to a more genuine virtue. As one might put it in old-fashioned terms, reflection on apparent virtue leads us to real virtue.

SYNTHETIC A PRIORI JUDGMENTS

The problem referred to and then seemingly dropped at the beginning of paragraph 10, the problem of the real and the apparent world, received the most influential treatment in Nietzsche's recent heritage from Immanuel Kant. The next paragraph focuses on Kant. Nietzsche diagnoses Kantianism as the symptom of a psychic need to overcome sensualism. Kant's putative moral victory over sensualism and the apparent world consists in the invention of a moral synthetic a priori, the categorical imperative. Nietzsche skillfully parodies Kant's teachings on the synthetic a priori as an effort to answer a philosophic question by reformulating it, "with such a display of German profundity and curlicues" that no one before Nietzsche noticed what a monstrous ruse he had perpetrated: "'How are synthetic judgments a priori *possible*?' Kant asked himself—and what really is his answer? 'By virtue of a faculty'" (*Vermöge eines Vermögens*, which is more obviously ludicrous than the English, p. 208). This imputation to Kant, which has the form of a joke, has a serious basis. For whence does the table of categories, on which synthetic a priori judgments are grounded, derive? Is it not true that Kant simply observes the predicates of speech and then classifies them a posteriori? And is not this classification "internalized" into man's permanent mental apparatus by Kant's effective knighting ceremony in the *Critique of Pure Reason*? Thus in Nietzsche's view, Kant fails to answer the superficial question he does see, namely how synthetic a priori judgments are possible, and fails even to discern the deeper question of why belief in such judgments is necessary for human beings. Nietzsche's answer to this deeper question is that good life is impossible without synthetic judgments a priori, however false these judgments might be (p. 209). On this question Nietzsche commits a gross injustice against Kant, who would be the last to overlook the necessity to believe in constructions for the sake of good human life; indeed, we may wonder whether Nietzsche inherits this insight precisely from Kant. In any case, in conceding that synthetic judgments a priori are necessary for human life, does Nietzsche not implicitly grant that man cannot live with a world of total flux?

SOUL AS SUBJECTIVE MULTIPLICITY

In the twelfth paragraph Nietzsche adverts from Kant's "real world" to the world of the senses. He recounts how the scientists Copernicus and Boscovich have undermined the evidence of the eyes (*Augenschein*) by persuading us to believe—he does not say "by demonstrating"—that the earth moves and that the atom as a particle of earth does not exist.[55] Just as we cannot know the truth of the "real world," so we cannot know the truth of the "apparent world." What about within ourselves? Nietzsche next asserts that belief in the human soul as an indestructible, eternal, indivisible monad ought to be eliminated from science, though he does wish to continue to speak of "the soul." For him "the soul" will refer to a "subjective multiplicity," i.e., the "social structure of the drives and affects" (p. 210). Unlike earlier notions of the soul, Nietzsche's "mortal soul" is not essentially rational and thus partakes of limited intelligibility. The scientist who adopts a Nietzschean understanding of the soul accordingly condemns himself to invention (*sich zum Erfinden verurteilt*, p. 211). But Nietzsche surmises that his new psychologist perhaps therewith also opens the door to discovery (*Finden*), i.e., to new truths, which he could not have reached in either the noumenal or the phenomenal world as conceived before Nietzsche.

THE WILL TO POWER AS DISCHARGE OF STRENGTH AND SELF-OVERCOMING

The central paragraphs of the first chapter are 12 and 13.[56] Paragraph 13 expressly continues the introduction of the will to power. This especially serious paragraph immediately follows the playful pun on *Erfinden* and *Finden* at the end of paragraph 12. At first glance, Nietzsche appears to change the subject in the thirteenth paragraph, but on reflection we notice that the will to power is essential to his allegedly novel "soul as subjective multiplicity." The pun at the end of the twelfth paragraph is also very suggestive as a potential ligature into the thirteenth: Nietzsche is probably indicating that the doctrine of the will to power is paradoxically both his invention and his discovery. He asserts in paragraph 13 that the drive for self-preservation ought not to be posited as the cardinal drive of living things, because actions directed at self-preservation are mere epiphenomena of the fundamental will to power. As a part of this challenge to the classical moderns, he argues that the drive for self-preservation is a superfluous teleological principle. He implies that one can, at least in principle, fully explain an organism's efforts to preserve itself in terms of its will to discharge its strength; but one cannot give a comprehensive explanation of an organism's efforts to discharge its strength in terms of its drive for self-preservation. Since Nietzsche professes allegiance to the rule of sparseness of principles, indeed since method *must* be essentially sparseness of principles (*wesentlich Prinzipien-Sparsamkeit sein muss*), the doctrine of the will to power has superior explanatory value (p. 211). But why should there be only one basic principle for any given explanation? Why not two, why not a hundred thousand? Nietzsche does not elaborate, but it hardly requires prodigies to answer for him. He quite properly relies on the principle of noncontradiction: a phenomenon has not been explained at all if it is "explained," simultaneously and in the same respect, in terms of "x" and in terms of "not x." Hence if there are two "explanatory" principles, the connection between them must also be explained, i.e., the two must be reduced to one. Ergo, the argument for the superiority of the doctrine of the will to power as an explanatory device presupposes the primacy of the principle of noncontradiction. This dependency can be reformulated in such a way as to make its paradoxical character more vivid: the insight into radical supremacy of the irrational in the human economy depends upon the primacy of reason.

Nietzsche is characteristically terse in his treatment of the will to power in paragraph 13. He does not make it clear why one cannot adequately account for an organism's effort to discharge its strength in terms of its drive for self-preservation. One can clarify this issue by drawing upon *Thus Spoke Zarathustra* for the Nietzschean teaching on self-overcoming. The will to power is indistinguishable from the will to self-overcoming, a will to overcome a self that is radically imperfect but longs to move toward perfection.[57] Perfection, however, is not only unattainable—it is unfixed. Thus, according to the doctrine of the will to power, the history of a self is an uninterrupted series of insurrections against the self, insurrections paradoxically led by what in the self is predominant, the will to power. Even in the late twentieth century this doctrine is so strange to our ears that, in order to convey it, at least one well-informed scholar understandably translates "*der Wille zur Macht*" as "the will to overpower."[58] In contrast to this doctrine of the will to overpower, the classical-modern teaching asserts that the self wants not to replace, overturn, or transcend, but to *maintain* itself. Hobbes, Locke, and Spinoza seem to presuppose a certain completeness in the self that Nietzsche finds metaphysically ludicrous and morally distasteful. Nietzsche takes it to be a fact that living things strive, and men in their humanity strive consciously, to rise above themselves, a fact for which the early moderns fail to take due provision. Were Aristotle allowed to enter this fray, he would undoubtedly agree that at least men in their developed humanity do strive for something higher than themselves. Yet he would complain against Nietzsche and the early moderns alike that the perfection for which men strive must somehow be fixed by nature for it to be intelligible. Even a variety of languages testify to the connection between rendering something intelligible and holding it in a fixed position: when we do not understand something, we say we do not comprehend or grasp (*begreifen, lambanein, katalambanein, accipere, comprendre*) it. Nietzsche's doctrine of self-overcoming thus obliges him to show what appears to be indemonstrable, that change directed at a fluxional goal can be *ascending* change or *overcoming*. (Cf. pp. 42–47, "The Ego and the Will," and pp. 49–50 below.)

THE DEBUNKING OF PHYSICS

Having dethroned the "drive for self-preservation" in the domain of universal explanation, Nietzsche in paragraph 14 continues his debunking effort by exposing physics as mere interpretation. He unexpectedly duplicates this exercise a bit later in the chapter (*BGE* 22). An additional treatment of physics may be warranted because it is the science of nature and nature is so very important for Nietzsche, but it goes without saying that a second visit must yield insights not available during the first. Each of the paragraphs on physics has two discernible parts, and in each the first part presents modern physics in an unfavorable light, whereas the second part offers a much more attractive alternative. In paragraph 14 modern physics is attacked as plebeian because its most fundamental presupposition is "eternally popular" sensualism (pp. 211–12). In paragraph 22 modern physics is again attacked as plebeian, this time because physics subjects everything to the same laws and thus equalizes all things (p. 220). In both cases physics operates on a mere prejudice, which the physicists naively fail to recognize as such, and in both cases that prejudice is vulgar and hence loathsome to Nietzsche. Modern physics is animated by the desire to abolish the distinctions between the noble and the base, the sacred and the profane, the desire to reduce all things to the same level. Appropriately, paragraph 14 contrasts with the repulsiveness of vulgar modern physics "the charm of the Platonic way of thinking, which was a noble (*vornehm*) way of thinking, [and which] consisted precisely in resistance to obvious sense-evidence—perhaps among men who enjoyed even stronger and more demanding senses than our contemporaries, but who knew how to find a higher triumph in remaining masters over these senses" (p. 212). Later, paragraph 22 replaces this alternative to modern physics with Nietzsche's own doctrine of the will to power. Although he does not call his doctrine noble, juxtaposition of the two paragraphs suggests what one could suspect in any case. In neither paragraph does Nietzsche attempt actually to refute modern physics through argument; he proceeds as though his charge of ignobility offers sufficient refutation.

SENSUALISM

Paragraph 14 concludes with something of a riddle, which paragraph 22 unriddles. At the end of paragraph 14 Nietzsche remarks that sensualism may be exactly the right teaching for the machinists and bridge builders of the future (ibid.). Why does he not simply abandon ignoble sensualism for something noble like Platonism? Up to the last sentence everything in the paragraph seems aimed at a total rejection of sensualism. But the explanation has already been indicated: Nietzsche believes that with the doctrine of the will to power and its accouterments, he can promulgate a teaching that is both sensualistic and noble.

There occurs in the fourteenth paragraph another paradox, which is treated in the fifteenth. Nietzsche begins paragraph 14 with the contention that physics is but interpretation and with the clear implication that sensualism, the premise of physics, is also mere interpretation. At the close of the paragraph, however, he suggests that the operational assumption of sensualism, "where man cannot find anything to see or to grasp, he has nothing more to seek" (ibid.), must be the imperative for men of the future. Since what is acknowledged publicly as a mere construction cannot readily serve as an imperative for anyone, he speaks in favor of sensualism in

BGE 15. His argument on its behalf is directed against those, un-named and doubtless few in number, who maintain that the external world is the work of our organs. Inasmuch as our organs are a part of the external world, and since we posit that our organs can-not be the cause of themselves,[59] the external world cannot be the work of our organs, *Q. E. D.* (pp. 212–213). If the external world is not the work of our organs, then presumably our senses convey information about precisely the external world, and so sensualism is vindicated. But Nietzsche leaves this vindication to be deduced by the reader, and he himself ends with a question mark that points to a defect in the argument. Our assumption of the absurdity of a *causa sui* leads only to the conclusion that *that part* of the external world that our organs constitute is not the work of our organs. Whether the external world at large is the work of our organs has not been established one way or the other. No wonder, then, that in paragraph 15 Nietzsche still calls sensualism a *hypothesis*.

THE EGO AND THE WILL

In the next four paragraphs, 16 through 19, Nietzsche dissects the ego and the will. Most obviously he attacks such moderns as Descartes and Schopenhauer, but he criticizes them not so much for their modernity as for their Platonizing. "There are still harm-less self-observers who believe there are 'immediate certainties'; for example, 'I think,' or, as the superstition of Schopenhauer was, 'I will,' just as if knowledge (*das Erkennen*) here got hold of its ob-ject purely and nakedly as 'the thing in itself,' without any falsifi-cation on the side of either the subject or the object" (*BGE* 16, p. 213). What rankles Nietzsche here is that with respect to the human internality the moderns naively believe that the *pure spirit* can ap-prehend immediate certainties and absolute knowledge (*absolute Erkenntnis*), and that the so-called certainties supposedly appre-hended by the moderns are abstractions from the body. He attempts to overthrow the tyranny of the Platonic conception by revealing its contradictory character, exposing its many unexamined presup-positions, and substituting in its place the first thoroughly corpore-alized human personality. Nietzsche puts the ego and the free will into one disposable Platonic package and replaces them with the self. Then he tells us, somewhat mysteriously, that the self is the body, that the body is the self. Nietzsche's "mortal soul," which was first encountered in paragraph 13, is mortal because it is absolutely bodily.

Nietzsche asserts that the "immediate certainty" that Descartes attaches to the thinking ego and Schopenhauer ascribes to the will is an expression that involves a *contradictio in adjecto*, a contradiction between the noun and the adjective; one can be certain of something, if ever, only *after* subjecting it to the severest scrutiny. Here again Nietzsche relies, this time explicitly, on the principle of non-contradiction for distinguishing between the sensible and the absurd.[60] Let us reconsider that principle in the present context. If the criterion of sensibleness is noncontradiction, and if that criterion cannot be persuasively supported by arguments that presuppose it (since such arguments would beg the question), must not the principle of noncontradiction itself qualify as an immediate certainty? Perhaps some follower of Nietzsche would deny the possibility of immediate certainty even in this case and describe the principle as a "shared prejudice." But does a principle common to all civilized men in all ages up to and including the present, deserve to be called a mere "prejudice"?[61] Nietzsche might insist that the principle is often useful for life and *therefore* valid. Once we become fully conscious of this justification, however, does it not follow that whenever the principle of noncontradiction is detrimental to life and hence invalid, it can and should be abandoned? (We might keep this question in mind when we come to the affirmation of the eternal recurrence). Yet following this line of thought would lead us to conclude that the principle of noncontradiction itself is no criterion at all—without any regard for the *"contradictio in adjecto,"* we must reject "immediate certainties" and "absolute knowledge" solely because they frustrate "life." In other words, since life equals the creative will, and since anything absolutely fixed or certain limits creativity, immediate certainties and absolute knowledge must be denied for the sake of the fullest imaginable creativity rather than for the sake of consistency. One might accuse Nietzsche of relying on his own so-called immediate certainty when he proclaims that life is creativity, but Nietzsche can always rejoin that he sets forth the doctrine of the will to power as interpretation, not as text (*BGE* 22, pp. 220–21).

When he turns to particular "certainties," Nietzsche first assaults the seeming certainty of the experience of one's own thinking. The sentence "I think," which expresses this experience, assumes the concept "ego," one's own particular ego as the individual agent, cause and effect, and the substantive meaning of thinking that distinguishes it from other experiences such as feeling (*BGE* 16, p. 213). To Nietzsche's mind the fact that there are presuppositions at all in the certainty of the sentence "I think" renders the *immediate* certainty of "I think" dubious, and certainly the last presupposition named explodes the possibility of immediate certainty of one's own thinking. Distinguishing between thinking and willing or feeling requires comparisons between and among one's present and previous activities and experiences. No matter how certain one might become of the reliability of those comparisons, one cannot accurately call that certainty "immediate" (ibid.). The reader should take care not to grant Nietzsche too much on the basis of the very penetrating argument here. He has established that the experience of one's own thinking lacks immediate certainty. But he has by no means proven either that all immediate certainties are impossible or that one's experience of one's own thinking is uncertain—the mediated certainty of one's experience of "I think" might simply depend upon prior certainties, perhaps even some certainties that are indeed immediate. We can anticipate, however, Nietzsche's complaint that the assumption of causality, for example, introduces not just an uncertainty but a fiction into the sentence "I think," for Nietzsche takes for granted the cogency of Hume's critique of causality.

> One should not wrongly reify "cause" and "effect," as the natural scientists do (and whoever, like them, now "naturalizes" in his thinking), according to the prevailing mechanical doltishness that makes the cause press and push until it "effects" its end; one should use "cause" and "effect" only as pure concepts, that is to say, as conventional fictions for the purpose of designation and communication—not for clarification (*Erklärung*). In the "in-itself" there is nothing of "causal connections" . . . ; there the effect does not follow the cause, there no "law" rules. It is we alone who have fabricated (*erdichtet*) cause [*BGE* 21, p. 219].

It is noted in passing that Nietzsche's denial of causality requires of him a reliable vision of the noumenal world, the world not as it appears to us but as it is absolutely apart from us, "in itself." At any rate it is fair to ask whether Nietzsche's central metaphysical doctrine of the will to power does not presuppose (willful) cause and (willed) effect. However difficult it may be to assign a *specific* cause to a *specific* effect, is it not impossible to speak intelligibly, or even to think, about the world of becoming without in some way presupposing cause and effect? Is an effect absolutely without a cause any more imaginable than a squared circle?[62] If not, why should we not take for granted, at least barring powerful new evidence, that neither causeless effects nor square circles exist? At a minimum it would seem that the principle of cause and effect remains impregnable to the will's effort to create and destroy.

In paragraph 17 Nietzsche continues the demolition of the ego that he began in paragraph 16. Now he replaces the thinking ego with a proto-Freudian id, for the assumption that "I" think is nothing more than a mere supposition, "to put it mildly." Nietzsche says "to put it mildly" because in fact he considers the belief in the "I" to be a grave error, since that belief accords neither with love of the earth, i.e., strict corporealism, nor with the doctrine of the will to power, i.e., thoroughgoing creativity or self-overcoming. Moreover, even the belief in the id rests on an interpretation and does not derive from an unbiased perception of the process of thinking itself (p. 214). Even the statement "it thinks" presupposes cause and effect, and Nietzsche suggests that rigorous minds (*Köpfe*) will abandon both cause and effect and even the id (p. 214). As previously remarked, Nietzsche does not entirely jettison cause and effect when he propounds the doctrine of the will to power, however, and other readers are invited to rise to the challenge of distinguishing between the id and the Nietzschean bodily self. If it should turn out that the fully developed Nietzschean self can arrive at truths by nature, truths regarded as noninterpretive by that self, perhaps one could argue that the Nietzsche self differs from the id precisely by its similarity to the ego. But between the id and the subjective multiplicity of the strictly corporeal self no difference can be found.

With the demise of the ego perhaps the theory of a "free will" also collapses, for can the will correctly be called free if the self is strictly corporeal? Nietzsche strongly repudiates the freedom of the will in paragraphs 18 and 19. In paragraph 18 he offers an exceptionally flippant psychological explanation of the persistence of the theory of a free will: men continue to find the theory attractive because they congratulate themselves on their strength when they manage to refute it. Nietzsche even remarks that it seems that the theory would not persist at all were it not for that attraction (pp. 214–15). If indeed the theory of a free will is erroneous, it seems far more likely that its charm should be attributed to men's feeling of strength by virtue of their (imaginary) freedom, rather than to their feeling of strength over their capacity to endure unfreedom. One suspects Nietzsche knows very well that this psychology of the doctrine of free will is more likely accurate than the one he offers, probably tongue-in-cheek. His psychology of the doctrine, however, proves more revealing of Nietzsche's own psychic disposition toward the will, for in paragraph 19 he opens up a radical separation between willing and acting, to the effect that there may never be any nonimaginary connection between the two. A "whole series of erroneous conclusions, and consequently of false evaluations of the will itself, has become attached to the act of willing—to such a degree that he who wills believes sincerely that willing *suffices* for action. Since in the great majority of cases there has been exercise of will only when the effect of the command—that is, obedience; that is, the action—was to be *expected*, the *appearance* has translated itself into the feeling, as if there were a *necessity of effect*" (*BGE* 19, p. 216). Paragraph 19 can therefore be said to undermine the concept of the will to power, and Nietzsche intimates in paragraph 18 that concerning his own theory "he feels he is strong enough to refute it" (p. 215; cf. *BGE* 38–39, pp. 239–40 and our interpretation thereof below). To the attentive reader, Nietzsche makes it remarkably clear that his denial of freedom of the will includes a denial of the will to power, for he says that consciousness of its own freedom and of its superiority to him who must obey is inherent in every will (*BGE* 19, ibid.). The sense of one's free will, while illusory, is nonetheless healthy; in an extremely important passage Nietzsche compares the will's delight in its illusion of commanding to the condition of a well-built and happy commonwealth that cannot fail to remind us of the healthy political aristocracy discussed in the ninth chapter of *BGE* on nobility:

> It suffices [to say] that he who wills believes with a fair amount of certainty that will and action are somehow one; he ascribes the success, the carrying out of the willing, to the will itself, and thereby enjoys an increase of the sensation of power that accompanies all

success. "Freedom of the will"—that is the expression for the complex state of delight of the person willing, who commands and at the same time identifies himself with the executor of the order—who, as such, enjoys also the triumph over obstacles, but thinks within himself that it was authentically his will itself that overcame them. In this way the person willing adds the feelings of delight of his successful executive instruments, the useful "underwills" or undersouls—indeed, our body is but a social structure composed of many souls—to his feelings of delight as commander. *L'effet c'est moi*:[62] what happens here is what happens in every well-constructed and happy commonwealth (*Gemeinwesen*). In all willing it is absolutely a question of commanding and obeying, on the basis, as already said, of a social structure composed of many "souls." Hence a philosopher should claim the right to include willing in itself within the sphere of morals—morals being understood as the doctrine of the relations of lordship under which the phenomenon of "life" comes to be [pp. 216–17].

Nietzsche's doctrine of the will to power is itself perspectival and thus, from the point of view of traditional metaphysics, dubious. But his doctrine makes possible the *healthy* will, i.e., nobility. The doctrine of the will to power is the precondition for the moral revivification of humanity, to command by the high and obedience by the low. But what serves as the ultimate ground for the distinction between high and low, noble and base?

Just as it must be granted that Nietzsche demonstrates that recognition of one's own thinking is no immediate certainty, so must it be admitted that he shows that the singularity of the will is highly problematical. The main point of his demonstration will perhaps become clearer if we advert briefly to one of the ancient Greek equivalents for the word "will" (*Wille*), namely "*proairesis*" or "forechoice." Aristotle defines "forechoice" as "deliberative appetite," or "thinking appetite," or "appetitive mind."[63] Now it is all very well for Aristotle or for various modern thinkers to join together two quite different elements of the soul under one heading such as "forechoice" or "will," provided only that they can explicate the ground of the unity of the apparently divergent elements. But Nietzsche's point is that the unity of that manifold will cannot be established. The concepts "will" and "free will" are mere locutions—and insofar as convictions attach to them, mere prejudices.

HISTORY AND NATURE

If one had to place paragraphs 12–19 under one heading, it would
probably have to be something like "Nietzsche's Corporealization
of the Soul," for in that portion of the chapter he erects his physiopsychology. In paragraph 20 Nietzsche reveals for the first time in
BGE that his physiopsychology is historicist. Against John Locke,
who in his *Essay on Human Understanding* argues that ideas originate from sensory impressions, and thus also against Thomas
Hobbes, whose position in Part I of the *Leviathan* and elsewhere
Locke attempts to perfect—and, of course, against the unmentioned
Plato and Aristotle, who are famous for teaching that the ideas are
eternal rather than historical—Nietzsche argues that philosophical
concepts derive from the historical development of language (*BGE*
20, pp. 217–18). Concepts do not grow capriciously or au-
tonomously (*nichts Für-sich-Wachsendes*) as Locke seems to think,
for they are all a part of a huge system of thought. Again and again
the most diverse philosophers fit into "a definite fundamental
scheme of possible philosophies" (p. 217), because of their development out of the original comprehensive household of the soul.
Indian, Greek, and German philosophy are *predictably* similar, because of their unconscious subordination to certain common grammatical functions, which dispose thinkers in some directions and actually prohibit others. Grammar is *decisive* for ideas because sense
data are ineluctably colored by the grammatical functions. Nietzsche adds that these functions express certain physiological and
racial conditions. But apparently grammatical functions do not develop rationally. Nietzsche's historicism partakes of the familiar difficulty of doctrines that attempt to immerse human thought irre-
trievably into historical process, the reflexive difficulty of the lack
of an absolute moment. In order to view the comprehensive household of the soul in its comprehensiveness, in order to capture the decisive truth of the historical ebb and flow, Nietzsche would need to
escape the inexorable limits of grammatical functions.

We have already noticed that in the next section, paragraph 21,
Nietzsche shows his awareness of the central problem of historicism
by claiming to know what the "in itself" is like. Despite the apparent
disjunction between paragraphs 20 and 21, they are actually tightly
bonded: the former points to a need for an absolute moment that the

latter supplies. Nietzsche's absolute insight into the world in itself reveals that apart from logical fictions, the following do not exist: causal connections, necessity, law, sequence, relation, constraint, number, freedom and unfreedom, ground, and purpose (p. 219). Were one reminded of substance in Spinoza's *Ethics*, one might be tempted to observe that Nietzsche completes the deanthropomorphization of the world that Spinoza unsuccessfully tries to universalize.[64] But to be truer to Nietzsche, it must be emphasized that he does not call the "in itself" a "world" at all. "The things" (*die Dinge*) become world only when we project and mix our own symbols into the things, and this transformation into "world" accomplished by human beings amounts to mythologizing. Put otherwise, the "world" (he does not say the "in itself") "viewed from the inside, the world defined according to its 'intelligible character' . . . would be 'will to power' and nothing else" (*BGE* 37, p. 238; cf. *The Will to Power* 1067 and 1066). Apparently there is a kind of dualism in Nietzschean metaphysics between the things in themselves and the world as it is upon being created by the human will. Concerning the "in itself" Nietzsche can only give a negative description as above: the things do not have causal connections, necessity, law, sequence, and so on. It is impossible to provide a positive content for "the things." It is no coincidence that Nietzsche uses some form of "nature" three times in this paragraph, the first repetitious use since paragraph 9 on the Stoics.[65] "Nature" is again thrice repeated in the following paragraph, *BGE* 22. The explanation may well be that in a very deep sense the "in itself," the "things," and "nature" are for Nietzsche synonymous. In this sense nature is a "given" that is prior to the will to power. But this nature "in itself" is meaningless, and it cannot become meaningful until it receives the imprint of the will to power. Thus nature in its intelligibility is the will to power; one nature is added to another. As becomes especially clear in the *Twilight of the Idols*, Nietzsche attempts to carry this treatment of nature one step further.[66] Inasmuch as the first "nature," the "in itself," is unintelligible prior to the action of the will to power, the will to power becomes nature "in itself," and the activity of the will is creation in the strict sense, creation ex nihilo. One might say that Being and the will to power become indistinguishable. However, Nietzsche finds himself incapable of making this final step successfully, i.e., he finds it impossible to abolish nature as a "given" prior to the will to power.

The ambiguity that remains accounts for much of the wavering that one notices over and over again in Nietzsche's writings.

It is recalled from paragraph 19 that consciousness of freedom of the will is inherent in every will. The healthier the will, the more it delights in the feeling of commanding. One aspect, at least, of Nietzsche's doctrine of the will to power thus incorporates the *longing* for freedom of the will, even though that doctrine includes a denial that freedom of the will can be a fact. Thus the doctrine of the will to power involves a desire to be *causa sui* (cf. *BGE* 9), which at the beginning of paragraph 21 Nietzsche calls a self-contradiction, a logical rape and perversion (*Unnatur*, p. 218).[67] Nature is a standard for judging the *causa sui* and hence for judging the propounder of the doctrine of the will to power. But whereas nature is required for truth, the doctrine of the will to power is required for health. If nature does not conduce to health, nature must be replaced by will. Nietzsche effects this replacement in paragraph 22.[68] Of course, the elimination of nature in this sense destroys the possibility of an absolute moment. "Supposing that this [teaching that nature is will to power] also is only interpretation— and you will be eager enough to make this objection?—well, so much the better" (*BGE* 22, pp. 220–21).

TRANSCENDENCE OF
MORAL PREJUDICES AND FEARS

In the final paragraph of Chapter 1, Nietzsche encapsulates his position under the title of psychologist of the doctrine of the development of the will to power. He indicates that his effort is revolutionary in the strict sense by reminding us that for Plato, too, psychology is queen of the sciences, so in this respect Nietzsche as it were calls for a return to Plato (*BGE* 23, p. 222, cf. *BGE* 280, p. 414.) At the same time Nietzsche credits himself with absolute novelty, for no one has ever even come close to understanding psychology as the historical morphology of the will to power, thanks to their remaining hung up (*hängen geblieben*) on moral prejudices and fears (p. 221). His own psychology will sail right over morality, even if it means destroying his own morality, for the sake of depth (ibid.). (In this sense the highest for him, as for the ancients, is also the deepest.) However, since willing itself should be included within the sphere of morals (*BGE* 19, p. 217), we are entitled to say that Nietzsche's psychology actually replaces previous moralities with a new and more profound one.

What Nietzsche means by his psychology is not transparently easy to comprehend. He does call Stendhal the last great psychologist (*BGE* 39, p. 240; *BGE* 254, p. 384). So one might suppose that concentrated study of Stendhal would yield treasures, but ultimately Nietzsche could learn nothing even from Stendhal.[69] The unqualifiedly greatest psychologist before Nietzsche is Dostoevsky, the reading of whose writings Nietzsche regards as one of the most beautiful activities of his life. Dostoevsky is a profound human being who discovers while living among tough criminals in Siberia that those convicts are "carved out of just about the best, hardest, and most valuable wood that grows anywhere on Russian soil."[70] Dostoevsky is thus a psychologist who understands that nobility is beyond good and evil—he knows that the "Catilinarian existence" is the precursor to every Caesar.[71] Unfortunately for the student of psychology, Nietzsche in his books says very little else about Dostoevsky. Nietzsche does tell us in *The Antichrist* that Doestoevsky could have perceived well the charming mixture of sublimity, sickliness, and childishness in the Christian Redeemer type, and Walter Kaufmann may be right to contend that Nietzsche sees Jesus of Nazareth as a type of Dostoevskian idiot.[72] Also, in the unpublished notes that were later collected into *The Will to Power*, Nietzsche informs us that Dostoevsky, like Nietzsche, is a pessimist, but—also like Nietzsche—one with an instinct for power and magnificence.[73] Yet this information, even supplemented by occasional remarks in the literary remains, does not suffice to carry us very far. Fortunately, though, Nietzsche identifies the novel he considers Dostoevsky's principal work: *Crime and Punishment*.[74] A brief look at that work with the Nietzschean psychologist in mind, might therefore have some value.[75]

The general plot of *Crime and Punishment* can be summarized as the story of the protagonist's short excursion beyond good and evil and of the awesome destruction unleashed upon him as a result, ostensibly because he is a defective human being. (The "happy ending" of the epilogue that follows Rodion Raskolnikov's confession to his two acts of murder is so palpably phony as to alert every competent

critic to the likelihood of Raskolnikov's suicide rather than his con-
version, and Dostoevsky wrote an alternative ending in which
Raskolnikov does kill himself.) The text is peppered with such observations as that "facts are not everything—at least half the business
lies in how you interpret them," and that being oneself is extremely
important, probably the most important thing of all.[76] Raskolnikov,
himself a rather perspicacious psychologist in Dostoevsky's eyes,
"does not like showing his feelings, and would rather do a cruel thing
than open his heart freely"; we can only be reminded of *Twilight of
the Idols*, where Nietzsche remarks that it would be an unworthy act
for a great soul to express the confusion that it feels.[77] Raskolnikov
advances the doctrine that there are but a few great men out of the
vast multitudes of human beings, and for these few the most infa-
mous crimes are altogether justifiable. He tends to think of Napoleon
as the prime example, but we might just as easily be reminded of Cesare Borgia, or of Romulus. At any rate, all life, for Raskolnikov, is
a preparation for this superior type and *ought* to be in abject servitude
to these great men. In the last quarter of the book suffering is glori-
fied, but at the same time the thought is expressed that the man who
lives most joyously is the most adept at self-deception.[78] The epilogue, which as already asseverated is manifestly unsatisfactory, suggests via the main character that only through the self-deception of
religious faith can a thoughtful man escape his profound awareness
that his life is not worth living. At the least, attention to Dostoevsky
can add to our information about the psychological objects that really
interest Nietzsche. If we now limit ourselves to drawing a single
risky generalization about the Nietzschean psychologist, we might
venture to describe him as thoroughly dominated by his own will, totally free of prejudice and tradition, "free as a bird."[79] Nietzsche's
great psychologist is the "free spirit," and this fact provides the specific ligature from the end of chapter 1 to chapter 2.

HEGEL

We leave chapter 1 with one final consideration, a passing historical observation concerning one of Nietzsche's great teachers who
properly should be acknowledged. Hegel is never mentioned in the
first chapter—his name occurs only four times in the whole of

BGE—despite his enormous influence on the chapter and the book as a whole. Nietzsche's debts to Hegel include the crucial doctrine that all human thought is historically bound and the abolition of the ego—for Nietzsche the subject and the ego are synonomous—so one can reasonably say that Nietzsche's anti-Platonism and anti-Hegelianism are built on Hegel's foundations.[80] Admittedly the contrast between their teachings is stark: on the surface pitting Hegel against Nietzsche amounts in many respects, both in style and in substance, to a confrontation of rationalism with romanticism. For Hegel, reason is supreme; for Nietzsche, passion or will is supreme. For Hegel, the science of knowledge produces a grand system of thought; for Nietzsche, the will to system building reflects a lack of probity. For Hegel, the state is reason incarnate, whereas in Nietzsche's eyes the state is the coldest of all cold monsters whose sign signifies the will to death.[81] The critical theoretical difference between the two would seem to be their positions on the possibility of an absolute moment. Nietzsche apparently believes that if there could be an absolute moment the pure mind and the good-in-itself would exist, so Platonism would win the decisive victory. In effect it is in order to avoid being caught by the ever-looming figure of Plato that Nietzsche struggles to free himself from Hegel's long tentacles. Yet out of his love of liberty, Nietzsche would disable the predatory jaws of History with the best weapon at his disposal, a well-honed sword of nature.[82]

THE PHILOSOPHIC LION

Chapter 2 is entitled "The Free Spirit." The subject matter of this chapter is more difficult to discern from either the title or the text than is the case in either the preceding or the following chapter. Chapter 1 rather clearly concerns the relationship between the philosophy of the future and the metaphysicians of all prior ages, and chapter 3 visibly treats the relationship between philosophy, especially the philosophy of the future, and religion. But what does this examination of the "free spirit" concern? One gets some help from the intimation that the believer in the eternal recurrence in chapter 3 is childlike (*BGE* 57, p. 259), and from the imagery of the beast of burden in chapter 1 (*BGE* 8, p. 205): chapters 1, 2, and 3 appear to parallel the familiar Nietzschean images of the camel, the lion, and the child, respectively. In all likelihood the free spirit thus corresponds to the lion in the "three metamorphoses" early in *Zarathustra*.[83] Zarathustra informs us that the lion cannot create new values, but the child can; in Chapter 3 the creative willing of the eternal recurrence is announced. But the lion that is incapable of creating values can nevertheless create freedom for itself for the sake of new creations. The lion must find deception and capriciousness even in things sacred in order to free itself from the old values.[84] The free spirit would seem to be an intermediate being, a precursor of the philosopher of the future, a forerunner whose existence is justified by the later advent of the affirmation of the eternal recurrence.[85] So the subject of the second chapter can be taken to be the freeing of the spirit from bondage to old values, the free spirit's liberation for the sake of creation. But this formula is so far unsatisfactory. Chapters 1 and 3 concern the relationship of philosophy to something else identifiable, and we still cannot identify what philosophy is juxtaposed with or related to in chapter 2. Analysis of the manifest content of chapter 2 reveals not one pervasive theme but several different ones: truth versus falsity, morality, solitude, esotericism, and the doctrine of the will to power. On close inspection, however, these topics can be seen to cluster around the venerable problem of the one and the many—indeed, this time the presentation of the doctrine of the will to power follows immediately after Nietzsche's vitriolic mockery of Voltaire's humanitarian search for truth in order to do the good (*BGE* 35 and 36, pp. 237–38). Accordingly, one can treat the subject matter of Chapter 2 as the relationship of philosophy to the unphilosophic multitudes.[86]

The title of chapter 2, "The Free Spirit," refers to one thing for the multitudes throughout Europe and America and to another for Nietzsche (*BGE* 44, pp. 244–46). To the many the free spirits are *libres-penseurs, liberi pensatori, Freidenker*, what in Nietzsche's time and still are called "free thinkers" (ibid., p. 244). In marked contrast to these slaves of the democratic taste and advocates of "modern ideas," Nietzsche's free spirits eschew all lures to spiritual dependence (ibid., p. 245). Nietzsche even includes himself among the genuine free spirits in the concluding paragraph of chapter 2 by speaking of "we free spirits" (ibid., pp. 244–46; cf. end of preface).[87] Thus the true free spirit is at least an inchoate philosopher, and every philosopher of the future will be a free spirit (ibid., p. 243). The subject of chapter 2 deserves to be called philosophic freedom in contradiction to the slavish, so-called freedom of the unphilosophic. Nietzsche is not merely making the traditional distinction between the philosophic human beings' liberation from opinion and others' ultimate enslavement to convention, however. All supposed "free spirits" who believe in truth as distinguished from appearance are far from being truly free, inasmuch as they are slaves to their faith in the truth.[88]

> When the Christian crusaders in the Orient encountered the invincible order of Assassins, that order of free spirits par excellence, whose lowest ranks followed a rule of obedience the like of which no order of monks ever attained, they obtained in some way or other a hint concerning that symbol and watchword reserved for the highest ranks alone as their *secretum*: "Nothing is true, everything is permitted." — Very well, *that* was *freedom* of spirit; in *that* way the faith in truth itself was abrogated.[89]

Only those strong enough to *assassinate* truth are free-spirited, and the falsely so-called free spirits are "more rigid and unconditional than anyone else."[90] Prior to Nietzsche no philosophers were genuinely free-spirited.

ENDORSEMENT OF THE FALSIFIED WORLD

In the opening paragraph of chapter 2, Nietzsche marvels at the falseness of the oversimplified human world.[91] Language in particular provides us with a world of opposites, whereas actually there are no opposites (*BGE* 24, p. 225). Science absolutely requires the foundation in ignorance that language provides, and therefore even science at its best strives to preserve the falsified world that language makes possible. Here again Nietzsche requires a vision of the "in itself" in order to judge of the falseness of the simplified, falsified world. Yet he himself apparently endorses, on behalf of "life," a cheerful affirmation of the falsified world over the "in itself."

This endorsement of the falsified world constitutes a provocation to traditional philosophers and their followers, so in the following paragraph (25) Nietzsche expostulates with them. The philosophers

question science and refuse to submit to the simplifications and fal-
sifications of ordinary human existence. Thus the philosophers are
out of step with scientists and with their fellow human beings generally. And thus they sacrifice themselves "for the truth's sake,"
which has a deleterious effect on their philosophizing and on their
souls. They become poisonous, crafty, and bad. Worst of all, they
become subject to moral indignation, which "stupefies, animalizes,
and brutalizes." Moral indignation signifies complete degeneration
in a philosopher, and is the sure sign that he is very far from the
truth. One can hardly doubt that Nietzsche is correct here—for any
"philosophers" who do indeed write primarily out of moral indignation. The image comes to mind of Ajax killing the sheep in Homer's
Iliad—philosophers like all other human beings are too human not
to be critically blinded by their indignation once it takes over, and
moral anger renders them not just foolish but self-destructive. However, Nietzsche does not recommend to the philosophers that they
avoid martyrdom by simply affirming the falsified world. Rather, he
urges first and foremost that the philosopher go into solitude, and
second that he retain his philosophical attitude of self-questioning
and his sense of humor (pp. 226–27). The second recommendation,
offered in passing, does not remain a major theme but is rather
dropped by the wayside as the chapter develops. One might wonder
whether, in spite of Nietzsche's own marvelous attitude of keen self-
criticism and multilayered irony, he doubts the ultimate attainability
of the detachment from oneself that would be necessary to keep self-
doubt and self-depreciatory laughter *sub specie aeternae* central to
one's thought. Or is the second point his truest one?

LOVE OF NEIGHBOR

The theme of solitude, on the other hand, is continued in the next
paragraph. It turns out that the philosopher does not need Nietzsche's encouragement to seek solitude if he is a "choice (*auser-
lesener*) human being," for every choice human being *instinctively*
seeks a citadel where he can escape the rabble (*BGE* 26, p. 227).
Nietzsche thus reminds us of Socrates's plebeian nature, for
Socrates reportedly loves discoursing in the marketplace for the
sake of what he learns there. Nietzsche's complaint against Socrates

is not that he goes down into the crowd in order to gain knowledge, for Nietzsche next urges that the man predestined for knowledge *must* go down. But to Niezsche's eyes Socrates seems to go to the agora altogether willingly, whereas the elevated man does so glistening "in all the colors of distress, green and gray with disgust, satiety, sympathy, gloominess, and loneliness" (ibid.). If we understand the implicit criticism of Socrates correctly, Nietzsche perhaps fails to attach sufficient weight to Socrates's remark in the *Lysis* that he has no friends.[92]

In any case, Nietzsche continues that mixing with the rabble for the sake of knowledge need not be a hopeless or interminable task, for there are insightful "cynics" among the rabble who provide the free spirit with shortcuts to knowledge. The cynics have especially good eyes—and noses—for discerning the circuitous operation of hunger, sexual lust, and vanity. Nietzsche condemns the cynics because of their baseness but respects them for their clear-sightedness and in some instances even for their profundity. The profundity of certain cynics contrasts sharply with the blind folly of the morally indignant, including the philosophers of old; indeed, the cynics are closer to the free spirits than are the philosophers, for both have a capacity for seeing into "what is" (*"dans ce qui est,"* BGE 39, pp. 239–40; also BGE 26, p. 225). We recall that the philosophers of old suffer from the "faith in the opposition of values" (*BGE* 2, p. 200; *BGE* 24, p. 225), and it occurs to us that that faith may be the deepest theoretical ground of their moral indignation (see *BGE* 34, p. 236). Again the question arises whether that faith in opposites can truly be overcome or whether it is inherent to human thought. Does thought ineluctably presuppose an opposition between true and false and an opposition between good and bad? Can radical "cynicism" be maintained?

Nietzsche seemingly changes the subject in paragraph 27, but his claim there to require subtle interpreters does serve to repudiate any readers crude enough to classify Nietzsche himself as a vulgar cynic on the basis of his remarks in paragraph 26. (Other readers making finer distinctions among cynics might have to resist the temptation to speak of an opposition between the vulgar and the refined.) And the reminder that Nietzsche does everything to make it hard to be understood follows hard on the heels of his attack on the indignant, "no one *lies* as much as the indignant do" (*BGE* 26, p. 229); perhaps

Nietzsche's disparagement of indignant falsehoods is no less in need of careful qualification than his appreciation of the cynics. This conjecture will bear fruit when we come to the eternal recurrence and Nietzsche's own apparent spirit of revenge; for poets also lie a lot.

ESOTERICISM AND THE
HOPE OF ETERNAL RECURRENCE

Paragraphs 27 through 30 all focus on the inaccessibility to the many of the thought and lives of the great, an old theme to which Nietzsche gives new meaning. He uses the expression "think and live" to emphasize that thought is not comprehensive of life, but the converse does hold. Nietzsche's thought and life are hard for others to grasp because they flow so very quickly, like the current of the Ganges. When speaking so directly of his own thought and life, Nietzsche recurs to a primordial language or *Ursprache* and compares himself to a rapidly streaming river outside of the West (*BGE* 27, p. 229). Conceivably we should even say "prior to" the West, and take the Ganges as the original birthplace of humanity. The tempo of Nietzsche's free-spirited thought resembles that of very few others; only Aristophanes, Petronius, Machiavelli, and Lessing are named as serious candidates. Even among them it becomes clear that for all his extraordinary gifts, Lessing, the only recent figure of the four and the only German, is inferior to the other three (*BGE* 28, pp. 230–31). Goethe cannot even compete. The presto of the great writers implies an endorsement of the world of becoming, and "makes everything healthy by making everything run" (ibid., p. 231). Some readers will wonder whether movement can be an end in itself rather than a means to a state of fulfillment or end, i.e., whether health as here portrayed deserves such esteem. At any rate, on account of the transfiguring presto of Aristophanes's free-spirited thought Nietzsche "*forgives* everything Hellenic for having existed" (ibid.). This expiation is not easily come by, for Nietzsche profoundly understands what a huge scandal ancient Greece, and especially Plato, perpetrated.[93] Plato went so far as to repudiate life (ibid.). Nietzsche thus finds himself in a position where saying Yes to becoming and life requires the affirmation of those in the past who said No to life. This paradox, to the extent it allows of solution, he solves by promulgating the doctrine of eternal recurrence: the past is rendered subject to the affirmative will by the will's affirmative willing of the past. Just as Plato would have found it difficult to endure life without Aristophanes (ibid.), so would a convinced Nietzschean find it hard to bear life without the eternal recurrence.

In paragraph 29 Nietzsche indicates that those rare human beings who achieve presto in their thought and lives manage to do so by dissevering their minds from all attachments to conventions. But such cutting of ties requires great strength, even recklessness, and once performed allows of no repair. Also, men bound by conventions cannot comprehend or sympathize with the unconventional man, so they will at best be unhelpful to him if he comes to grief. Thus the unconventional man, the free spirit, is exceedingly vulnerable (pp. 231–32). Accordingly, he must devise a means of communicating with the multitude on one level and simultaneously with other free spirits on his own level. Ergo, the topic of paragraph 30 is esoteric versus exoteric writing. The esoteric approach looks down from above, whereas the exoteric looks up from below. The esoteric is so high that it transcends even tragedy. To this point Nietzsche simply echoes the Platonic view of esotericism, according to which philosophy and high comedy are fraternal twins, each much taller than tragedy. The major novelty arises with an allusion to the eternal recurrence that intimates that only the teacher thereof can fully comprehend the peaks of esotericism: "and taking all the woe of the world into one—who could dare to decide whether its sight would *necessarily* seduce us and compel us to feel pity and thus double this woe?" (p. 232; cf. *BGE* 56, p. 258). Whereas hitherto the account of esotericism was reliable, the suggestion that all the woe of the world need not compel us to feel pity is dubious unless one can look down upon one's own woe as the experience of one's lower self. Later Nietzsche does indeed distinguish between the higher self, or creator, and the lower self, or creature, in man (*BGE* 225, p. 344). But we will discover that for Nietzsche even the higher self experiences intense suffering, suffering from which it evidently cannot be detached; Nietzsche admits that he feels pity for the higher self (ibid.). We are thus provisionally led to wonder— albeit in full awareness that lurking behind a mask may be yet another mask—if Nietzsche's view of the world is more tragic than

comic, if in his very presentation of the notion of esotericism, he es-
oterically adumbrates the esoteric character of his central teaching,
the eternal recurrence.[94]

FAITH AND MORALITY

The free spirit, as we have seen, leads a dangerous life because of
his faithlessness in the conventions. It is from this faithlessness
that the need of esotericism stems in the first place. Now the faith-
less man must be an older man, a mature man, for children incline
to a naive faith in the unconditional (*BGE* 31, p. 233).[95] Can the
genuine free spirit possibly have faith in the doctrine of the eternal recurrence just alluded to? Does not Nietzsche himself indicate
that that faith, too, is childlike (*BGE* 57, p. 259)? Whatever the
case, Nietzsche detects three stages of development from youth to
maturity, three logically developing phases that seem to have a
necessary dialectical movement and cannot fail to remind us of
Hegel.[96] Not only the individual but mankind as a whole are subject to a three-stage metamorphosis. In paragraph 32 Nietzsche
traces humanity's development from the pre-moral period,
through the era of morality, to the coming period of supramorality
that will have its inception in Nietzsche's thought (pp. 232–34). In
other words, he devises here a schema of the genealogy of morals
in which, overall, there is steady progress—despite "long struggles and vacillations"—toward a peak, and that peak is Nietzsche's overcoming of morality. Whether the overcoming of
morality does not itself require a new morality is not addressed, although we have ample reason to suppose it does. What is made explicit is that the free spirit must overcome morality in the traditional sense because adherence to morality is enslavement to
prejudice (p. 234). As if it needed to be said, Nietzsche adds that
the critique of morality includes the critique of unselfishness; man
is, after all, a fundamentally selfish animal (*BGE* 33, p. 235). The
critique of unselfishness undermines not just Christianity and the
categorical imperative but also "contemplation devoid of all interest" (ibid. and *BGE* 64, p. 269). Even the philosopher's preference
for truth over appearance is merely a moral preference, to be
doubted by the free-spirited man. The very supposition that there

is an opposition between "true" and "false" is unnecessary, for an alternative can be fashioned according to which there are only different degrees of apparentness. If anything is more ludicrous and offensive than pursuit of knowledge for its own sake, it is the search for the truth in order to do good (*BGE* 35, p. 237). At any rate, one is neither free nor mature until one acknowledges that one's world is absolutely selfish, absolutely imprinted with the stamp of one's own will.

The free spirit adheres to the hypothesis that the world in its intelligible character is will to power and nothing else (*BGE* 37, pp. 237–38). He supposes that the world of our desires and passions is the only one, and that the "material world" can be explained as a congeries of manifestations of these desires and passions. Method, which is to say economy of principles, demands that supposition (ibid.; cf. *BGE* 13, p. 211). Taken at face value, Nietzsche's argument has all the trappings of rigorous logic: cause and effect cannot occur, presumably, except among things having the same basic nature. For example, body can move, and be moved by, only body. So if will can act on the material world, the material world must be fundamentally will (or vice versa).[97] Barring universal corporealism, method further requires that all efficient forces be traced back to a single basic form of the will, namely the will to power (p. 238). Thus "[m]ethod in investigation is attained only when all moral prejudices have been overcome: — it represents a victory over morality — ."[98]

Some of Nietzsche's readers might suppose that this victory over morality is a victory of the low over the high, even of the devil over God. Nietzsche insists to the contrary that through the doctrine of the will to power, God becomes victorious over the devil (*BGE* 37, p. 238). Nietzsche takes this position playfully but also with great earnestness. He can be said to be justified in doing so because the doctrine of the will to power seems to imply a divine Creator with unlimited or nearly unlimited powers (cf. *BGE* 150, p. 280).[99] The creative powers of the creator are identical to his interpretive powers, for the world comes into being *as world* through interpretation. Some matter, some *nature*, is required prior to the act of interpretation, but that matter is totally unintelligible prior to interpretation. Thus the text finally disappears under the interpretation (*BGE* 38, p. 239), entitling Nietzsche to refer to the doctrine of the will to power as following "of course" or "naturally" ("*'Wille' kann natürlich nur auf 'Wille' wirken*," *BGE* 36, p. 238); the interpretation becomes the text. Yet he is still alluding to his doctrine of creative will to power at the end of paragraph 38—and therein is the ligature back to the preceding paragraphs—when he remarks that our awareness of the fictitious character of the world undermines our belief in the world (p. 239). This awareness of the truth that the world however understood is a fiction may make men evil and gloomy, but it is no less a truth for that reason. The free spirit must be strong and independent enough to bear the ugliness of truth (*BGE* 39, pp. 239–40). On the other hand, the contention that the doctrine of the will to power is God's victory over the devil suggests that that doctrine, when fully developed, constitutes Nietzschean religion. Is the free spirit too impious, after all, to have faith even in the will to power?

Nietzsche does not expect his presentation of the doctrine of the will to power and of its dubiousness to be understood, even by his closest intimates. Therefore, he masks the deepest meanings of that doctrine, including his "mortal danger" (*Lebensgefahr*), from the world.[100] He describes the mask as the proper disguise for the shame of a god, and suggests that the god's shame is evoked by the sight of his own love and extravagant generosity (*BGE* 40, pp. 240–41). Is Nietzsche himself this god? If so, what is his act of love and extravagant generosity? We already know in a very general way what his action is in *BGE* as a whole, namely to prepare the way for a philosophy of the future. Paragraphs 42 through 44 focus on the new breed (*Gattung*) of philosophers, and these paragraphs conclude this second chapter of the book. The very title of the work already offers a clue that Nietzsche considers his paternity and midwifery to the new philosophers to be his acts of great love for humanity, indeed *the* acts of love par excellence: for "what is done out of love always occurs beyond good and evil" (*BGE* 153, p. 280). One can wonder why Nietzsche should be ashamed of his love and generosity. Does he mean no more than that some fine things are far too beautiful to expose to the vulgar, that one should not cast one's pearls before swine? It is not shameful to love what is excellent; shame would be appropriate only if one loved one's own despite the paucity of excellence (see *BGE* 102, p. 274). Zarathustra in the work named after him rhapsodizes about his love of man for the sake of the superman, i.e., for the sake of the inchoate excellence in man, and Zarathustra declaims about his great nausea over the baseness of man.[101] We find Zarathustra's nausea readily intelligible, though he may sometimes fail to effervesce it sufficiently with the champagnes of comedy, or even to dilute it well with the salubrious waters of philosophic resignation. But again, how can his love of human excellence be shameful? Is the superman or philosopher of the future out of human reach, or is there some higher being than he? Is the superman unlovable because he is impossible or because he is imperfect? With respect to Nietzsche's love and generosity, one can also wonder why, on the basis of Nietzsche's teaching so far, one should love anything other than oneself. He has already exposed the excess of "charm and sugar in . . . feelings of 'for others,' 'not for myself'" (*BGE* 33, p. 235); evidently the free spirit should not be bound by love and generosity that are not readily reducible to self-love and self-gratification. It is thus appropriate that immediately after introducing the subject of great love and generosity (*BGE* 40, p. 240), Nietzsche makes explicit that the free spirit must not remain stuck to his own virtues and become as a whole the victim of some detail in him, such as his hospitality, which is the danger of dangers for superior and rich souls who spend themselves lavishly, almost indifferently, and exaggerate the virtue of generosity into a vice. One must know how to *conserve oneself* (*sich bewahren*): the hardest test of independence (*BGE* 41, p. 242). Would the genuine free spirit restrain his generosity and refrain from giving humanity the superman? Or is the superman a gift given more to the giver than to mankind the receiver?[102]

A CATALOG OF FREEDOMS

Nietzsche lists six bonds of enslavement that the free spirit is careful to avoid. With one exception, the list is a catalogue of freedoms that distinguish the free spirit from the multitude. The free spirit will remain attached to neither a person (not even the most loved), nor a fatherland, nor a pity (not even for higher men), nor a science, nor his own detachment, nor his own virtues such as generosity (*BGE* 41, p. 242). Whatever might be said of the possibility of the superman, certain it is that the free spirit can exist: Nietzsche implies that he himself is a free spirit, and on first and second scrutiny Socrates would seem to qualify, too. Especially as Nietzsche portrays him, Socrates's "ironic" marriage to Xanthippe is certainly no sign of the least psychic unfreedom—although one can wonder a bit about Nietzsche's relationship to Lou Andreas-Salomé.[103] Unlike Nietzsche, Socrates is no wanderer, but his indictment of Athens is quite as penetrating as Nietzsche's of Germany. The only "science" Socrates becomes attached to is philosophy, and he speaks of it more as a spiritual groping than as an ordered body of knowledge (*Wissenschaft*). Nietzsche's psychology is queen of the sciences, but "attachment" to *his* psychology is a sign of his freedom; moreover, he has in fact abandoned or transcended his original academic specialty, the science of philology. By "virtues" he apparently means what Aristotle called moral virtues, although our recollection of Nietzsche's reference to "the courage of the conscience" and to "probity" gives us pause. Socrates, at least, cannot in our view be convicted of remaining attached to moral virtues, which he regards as means to a higher end.[104] To the extent that Nietzsche arrives at a point beyond good and evil, he, too, can perhaps be said to be independent of his virtues.

The remaining sign of freedom, "not to remain attached to one's own detachment," is highly paradoxical. How can one scrupulously avoid attachments without being attached to one's avoidance of attachments? The fog begins to clear when it dawns on us that this requirement is probably designed to disqualify Socrates as a free spirit. Socrates is so monstrously rational and therewith detached from man's true, passionate nature that he requires a daimonion to restrain him.

We are offered a key to the character of Socrates by the wonderful phenomenon known as "the *daimonion* of Socrates." In exceptional circumstances, when his tremendous intellect wavered, he found secure support in the utterances of a divine voice that spoke up at such moments. This voice, whenever it comes, always *dissuades*. In this utterly abnormal nature instinctive wisdom appears only in order to *hinder* conscious knowledge occasionally. While in all productive men it is instinct that is the creative-affirmative force, and consciousness acts critically and dissuasively, in Socrates it is instinct that becomes the critic, and consciousness that becomes the creator—truly a monstrosity *per defectum*! Specifically, we observe here a monstrous *defectus* of any mystical disposition, so Socrates might be called the typical *nonmystic*, in whom, through a hypertrophy, the logical nature is developed as excessively as instinctive wisdom is in the mystic. But the logical urge that became manifest in Socrates was absolutely prevented from turning against itself; in its unbridled flood it displays a natural power such as we encounter to our awed amazement only in the very greatest instinctive forces. Anyone who, through the Platonic writings, has experienced even a breath of the divine naiveté and sureness of the Socratic way of life, will also feel how the enormous driving-wheel of logical Socratism is in motion, as it were, *behind* Socrates, and that it must be viewed through Socrates as through a shadow.[105]

In contrast to Socrates, Nietzsche's free spirit is no shadow. He is free of all bonds but one—the bond to his own passionate self. Nietzsche, like Socrates, is subject to "the danger of the flier," to the attraction of "that voluptuous remoteness and strangeness of the bird who flies ever higher to see ever more below him" (ibid.). But Nietzsche does not lose himself in outer space; Nietzsche, in contradistinction to Socrates, brings philosophy down to earth.

Unlike Nietzsche, we doubt that the *daimonion* ultimately stands for anything more than Socrates's practical wisdom, and thus suppose that Socrates is not so preternaturally detached as Nietzsche suggests. In our view Socrates would qualify as a free spirit at least as fully as Nietzsche would. But the *daimonion* can be presented as a separate entity because Socrates does strive at least as much as any other human being for a "detached objectivity," which radicalized to the extreme would entail an absurdly disinterested view of oneself. In this sense the *daimonion* is something superadded to the essential Socrates, and in this sense Nietzsche can understandably charge that his idealized Socrates is a slave to Socratic reason.[106] A follower of Socrates might rejoin that Nietzsche has constructed a defective ideal—a prudent Socrates is more reasonable than a Socrates lacking prudence—and that so-called slavery to dispassionate reason is far superior to any imaginable slavery to passion. Moreover, the Socratic turn to moral and political philosophy from so-called natural philosophy rests on the insight that the highest of all human concerns is to live a good life. Practical wisdom is thus central to Socrates's whole activity. Nietzsche so to speak Aristophanizes Socrates, who lived neither in a basket nor as a detached shadow. *Mutatis mutandis*, the free spirit Socrates forgot himself as little as "Mr. Nietzsche" did.

PHILOSOPHERS OF THE FUTURE

Nietzsche obviously has a high view of the free spirit, of him who supposedly stands even higher than Socrates, but for some reason he is compelled to think ahead to the philosophers of the future, who will be more than free spirits. Nietzsche ventures to "baptize" (*taufen*) the philosophers of the future attempters or experimenters (*Versucher*); the language of religion recalls the reference to God shortly before (*BGE* 37, p. 238; cf. *BGE* 2, p. 200) and points forward to the next chapter on the religious matter (*Wesen*). Since these philosophers of the future are Nietzsche's generous gift to humanity, and since they seem to represent Nietzschean religion, one might find in them cause to doubt Nietzsche's complete free-spiritedness. He tries to obviate such doubt by indicating that the philosophers of the future are actually only his experiment (*Versuch*) and his temptation (*Versuchung*) (ibid.) Moreover, he emphatically denies that the philosophers of the future will be dogmatic expounders of universal truths. Their truths will be "truths" peculiar to themselves, and the same applies to what they consider good (*BGE* 43, p. 243).

Nietzsche accordingly denies, in their name and in his own name, the possibility of a common good: "whatever can be common always has little value" (*BGE* 43, p. 243). Taken literally, the ridiculous character of this generalization could inspire a Voltairean satire: it suffices to mention the cardinal value for human life of pure food, clean air, and uncontaminated water. Like *Candide*, however, such a satire would miss the philosopher's main point, which in the present case is that even those common things necessary for preservation do not *ennoble*. The same applies to dealing with such things, or more generally with the common good. A grave objection arises: what about the aristocrat whose sense of self-worth and self-love depends upon the seriousness of his efforts to pursue the common good as a political leader? Nietzsche would accuse such a leader of ignobly identifying himself too closely with the interests of the vulgar, of being a traitor to his class (*BGE* 258, p. 392 and

BGE 287, p. 418). The true aristocrat sees himself and his like as the meaning and highest justification of his whole political order (ibid.) Life, after all, is essentially exploitative (*BGE* 259, p. 393).

Even if this assessment of the "common good" were sound, we have every reason to suppose that its public dissemination would have baneful effects upon philosophy however understood. Moreover, even the most monstrous tyrants need to pretend to rule on behalf of their subjects; unless Nietzsche's rulers can make the same public pretense, his political project will be doomed from the outset. At all events Nietzsche does first present his philosophers of the future as highly transpolitical: "In the end it must [continue to] be as it is and always was; great things remain for the great, abysses for the deep, nuances and shudders for the refined, and, in brief, all that is rare for the rare" (*BGE* 37, p. 238). Nevertheless, the two concluding paragraphs (43 and 44) concerning the philosophers of the future touch more directly on politics than any other paragraphs in the chapter. Precisely moral-political requirements may induce Nietzsche to advance from the free spirits to the philosophers of the future. The same requirements may also prompt him to complete the doctrine of the will to power with the teaching of the eternal return. In any case, Nietzsche feels a stronger obligation (*Schuldigkeit*) to himself and whatever other free spirits there may be than to the philosophers of the future, notwithstanding the ostensible superiority of the philosophers of the future (*BGE* 44, pp. 243–44).

Notes

1. *Twilight of the Idols*, "Skirmishes of an Untimely Man" 51, in *The Portable Nietzsche*, trans. and ed. Walter Kaufmann (New York: The Viking Press, 1968), p. 556. (Hereafter referred to as *Twilight* in *Portable Nietzsche*.) See also ibid., "How the 'True World' Finally Became a Fable," p. 486.

2. See Nietzsche's letter to Jakob Burckhardt, September 22, 1886, in *Selected Letters of Friedrich Nietzsche*, trans. and ed. Christopher Middleton (Chicago: University of Chicago Press, 1969), p. 255: "*Jenseits* . . . says the same thing as my *Zarathustra*—only in a way that is different—very different." *The Genealogy of Morals*, in turn, is an elaboration and completion of *BGE*. But the *Genealogy*, subtitled "A Polemic," is written on a more popular level and therewith necessarily distorts—especially nobility. We shall

therefore draw on the *Genealogy* at appropriate times as an important supplementary text, without devoting a separate treatment to it.

3. *Selected Letters*, p. 254.

4. Ibid.

5. *Ecce Homo*, *"Beyond Good and Evil,"* in *Basic Writings of Nietzsche*, trans. and ed. Walter Kaufmann (New York: Random House, Inc., The Modern Library, 1968), p. 767. (Hereafter referred to as *Basic Writings*.)

6. That the two disproportions are parallel can be seen by referring to ibid., p. 766. Just as, because of the dominance of the critique of modernity, the text of *BGE* appears to be less comprehensive than one would expect from the preface, so because of the emphasis on modernity does *BGE* seem much more restricted than *Thus Spoke Zarathustra*. If, as we contend, the critique of modernity should have much greater dimensions than strike one at first glance, both apparent disproportions would disappear.

7. See ibid.

8. Ibid.

9. That from the very beginning of *BGE* Nietzsche's effort to supplant Plato is, however, tentative rather than dogmatic, becomes evident when one takes note of the subtitle. Ludwig Feuerbach wrote a tract entitled *The Philosophy of the Future*, which Nietzsche changes to "Prelude to a *Philosophy of the Future*."

10. Quoted in Werner Dannhauser, *Nietzsche's View of Socrates* (Ithaca, N.Y.: Cornell University Press, 1974), p. 15. See also *The Gay Science*, trans. Walter Kaufmann (New York: Vintage Books, 1974), 340, p. 272.

11. *BGE* Preface, in *Basic Writings*, p. 193.

12. Ibid. Also ibid., 93, p. 273. Henceforth aphorism numbers of *BGE* will be included parenthentically, followed by the page number in *Basic Writings*. References to paragraphs indicate Nietzsche's, not Kaufmann's divisions.

13. *"Das religiöse Wesen,"* "The Religious Essence" in Kaufmann's rendition, might better be translated less literally as "The Religious Matter" or "What Is Going on in Religion." See Dannhauser, *Nietzsche's View of Socrates*, p. 182, n. 16. See also note 2 to chapter 3 below.

14. See the first essay of the *Genealogy of Morals*.

15. "In the end, my mistrust of Plato goes deep: he . . . is so moralistic, so pre-existently Christian—he already takes the concept 'good' for the highest concept—that for the whole phenomenon Plato I would sooner use the harsh phrase 'higher swindle' . . ." *Twilight*, "What I Owe to the Ancients," 2, in *Portable Nietzsche*, pp. 557–58.

16. Cf. Plato *Apology of Socrates* 30E.

17. *Twilight*, "The Problem of Socrates" 5, in *Portable Nietzsche*, p. 476.

18. See *BGE* 1–6, pp. 199–204.

19. Nietzsche avows that it is his ambition "to say in ten sentences what everyone else says in a book—what everyone else does not say in a book." *Twilight*, "Skirmishes of an Untimely Man" 51, in *Portable Nietzsche*, p. 556. The third essay of the *Genealogy of Morals* demonstrates that he considers his ambition—stated more directly, to write in ten sentences what all others would need a book to express if they could perceive what Nietzsche perceives, but of course they cannot—he considers his ambition fulfilled.

20. Nietzsche recognizes and adapts to this danger by following the tradition of esoteric writing. *BGE* 30, 40, and 289; *Human, All-too-Human* II, 2, "The Wanderer and His Shadow," 71; II, 1, "Mixed Opinions and Sayings," 338.

21. See the previous three notes.

22. On the other hand the writings of philosophers of nearly all stripes since early antiquity do rely on hints, asides, and mysterious apothegms.

23. *The Gay Science* 355, p. 301. The context makes it crystal clear that Nietzsche speaks of philosophy here, and thus of the will to truth. Cf. Hobbes, *Leviathan*, ed. Edwin Carley (Indianapolis, Ind.: Hackett Publishing Co., 1994) I, vi, p. 62.

24. In this regard Nietzsche's doctrine radicalizes Hobbe's teaching of the primacy of fearfulness in man. Conceivably such primacy may be true of Nietzsche himself. See, e.g., Martin Heidegger's essay "Who Is Nietzsche's Zarathustra?" *Review of Metaphysics*, 20, No. 79 (March, 1967), 414 ff.: Heidegger thinks he discerns in *Zarathustra* what "pervades the entire work" and "determines the style, the hesitant and constantly arrested course of the entire book," namely Nietzsche's *recoiling horror.* "One who has not previously and does not constantly perceive the horror in all the discourses—seemingly arrogant and often ecstatically conducted as they are—will never know who Zarathustra is."

25. See also *Twilight of the Idols*: "To derive something unknown from something familiar relieves, comforts, and satisfies, besides giving a feeling of power. With the unknown one is confronted with danger, discomfort, and care; the first instinct is to abolish these painful states. First principle: any explanation is better than none. Since at bottom it is merely a matter of wishing to be rid of oppressive representations, one is not too particular about the means of getting rid of them: the first representation that explains the unknown as familiar feels so good that one 'considers it true.' The proof of pleasure ('of strength') as a criterion of truth." "The Four Great Errors" 5, in *Portable Nietzsche*, p. 497. Fear of the unknown leads in this way not only to "the four great errors" but also to all so-called truths. Cf. *BGE* 192, pp. 294–95.

26. It pays to recall that the most famous appearance of a philosopher before accusers and law courts is the trial of Socrates. At the end of Plato's *Apology*, Socrates remarks that he goes to die and his audience remains to live; and which of them has the better fate, none unless the god—i.e.,

no one—knows. Since at least one philosopher, Plato, is in the audience, Socrates at the end of his apology might be expressing doubt about whether even philosophy makes life worth living. We cannot conceive of a larger question mark for Socrates to put after his special words and favorite doctrines. Nietzsche himself interprets Socrates's last words in the *Phaedo* to mean that life itself is a horrible sickness. *Twilight*, "The Problem of Socrates" 12, in *Portable Nietzsche*, p. 479. Nietzsche goes so far as to speak of the *wisdom* of Socrates's courage to die. Ibid. But cf. Plato's *Symposium* 204E–205A, Xenophon's *Symposium* ii. 19 and vii.1, and *Memorabilia* I. 6. xiv.

27. One can enhance one's reading of Nietzsche by identifying parts—divisions, chapters, paragraphs, parts of paragraphs—and inferring their connections. This method is especially appropriate for *BGE*, in which Nietzsche "'platonizes' as regards the 'form' more than anywhere else." See Leo Strauss, "Note on the Plan of Nietzsche's *Beyond Good and Evil*," *Interpretation* 4, No. 1 (Summer, 1974): 97–113; quotation taken from p. 97. When one has dialectically discovered the total skein of ligatures, one has as it were arrived at the whole truth of the work. The obverse of the dialectic of ligature construction is the dialectic of mask removal, for the interpreter of Nietzsche must expose and remove one layer of mask after another. Especially for the latter task, diligent scholarly labor alone will not suffice: one needs a well-developed sense of drama and irony. See Hans-Georg Gadamer, "The Drama of Zarathustra," trans. Thomas Heilke in Gillespie, *Nietzsche's New Seas*, pp. 220–31 and Jacques Derrida, *Spurs: Nietzsche's Styles* (Chicago: University of Chicago Press, 1978). See also David F. Krell, *Postponements: Women, Sensuality, and Death in Nietzsche* (Bloomington: Indiana University Press, 1986).

28. *The Birth of Tragedy* 9, in *Basic Writings*, p. 69. See also 3, 4, and 10.

29. Ibid., 3, p. 42.

30. See *BGE* 207, p. 318: "'*Je ne méprise presque rien*,' he says with Leibniz: one should not overlook and underestimate that *presque*." One might object as follows to our interpretation of Nietzsche's use of "almost" in the first paragraph: when Nietzsche qualifies his claim to originality, perhaps he does so because declaring oneself absolutely innovative exceeds the bounds of modesty. To such an objection we would rejoin that the author of "Why I Am So Wise," "Why I Am So Clever," and "Why I Write Such Good Books" in *Ecce Homo* does not typically indulge in self-depreciation. See also Jean-Jacques Rousseau, *The First and Second Discourses*, trans. Roger D. and Judith R. Masters (New York: St. Martin's Press, 1964), pp. 48–49: "The sciences and the arts owe their birth to our vices. . . . What dangers there are! What false paths! Besides who seeks

[truth] sincerely? . . . And hardest of all, if by luck we finally find it, who among us will know how to make good use of the truth?"

31. Nietzsche characterizes the metaphysics of all ages as "solemn baptizers" of the truth who subscribe to the faith in the opposition of values. See also *BGE* 5, p. 203.

32. See especially Book VI of the *Nicomachean Ethics* at 1140Aff.

33. The palinode is 243E–257B. See Joseph Cropsey's "Plato's *Phaedrus* and Plato's Socrates," in his *Political Philosophy and the Issues of Politics* (Chicago: The University of Chicago Press, 1977), pp. 231–51.

34. In the *Genealogy of Morals* I, 7, in *Basic Writings*, p. 469, Nietzsche says that man's depth and man's evil are the two basic qualities by which man has hitherto been superior to other beasts. Perhaps Nietzsche adds the qualifier "hitherto" because the last man, if he does inherit the earth, will be significantly superior in neither depth nor evil to the beast. In any case "depth" certainly means more than "acuteness of reason." Cf. *Genealogy* II, 8, p. 506.

35. "Real" comes from the Latin *res*, meaning "thing." Perhaps we should also notice that even the imaginary number system has utility for electrical engineering.

It is worthy of note that the meaning of the concept "number" may have changed in the 1500s. See Jacob Klein, *Greek Mathematical Thought and the Origin of Algebra*, trans. Eva Brann (Cambridge, Mass.: Massachusetts Institute of Technology Press, 1968). Since mathematical thinking is an instinctive activity according to Nietzsche, to explain any change in the meaning of the concept "number" one would have to give an account of why the passions governing mathematical thinking changed just when they did. Klein's more promising approach is to account for the change in the concept in terms of a rational thinking through of the nature of number.

36. Consider the image Plato employs in the *Republic* (516A-C): the philosopher leaves the cave and stares at the bright sun, i.e., the truth. Has Plato forgotten that actually staring directly at the bright sun melts one's eye tissues? Cf. the remarkable penultimate paragraph of *BGE*, namely 295, in which a god who resembles Socrates is said to have gone "further, very much further" than Nietzsche "in dialogues" and to have been "always many steps ahead of me." See *Zarathustra* II, "On the Famous Wise Men," where Nietzsche speaks of the blindness of the blind who looked into the sun. *Portable Nietzsche*, p. 216.

37. *Unschuld* can also suggest chastity, which might be important in terms of the imagery with which Nietzsche opens the preface.

38. Nietzsche's use of the term "*Gewissen,*" apparently as one of the notions that determine his thought, is striking. Is not the modern meaning of conscience inextricably bound up with "guilt," i.e., with the morality of good and evil? Cf. pp. 85–86 below.

39. See, e.g., note 24 above.

40. This study as a whole should lend support to the thesis proffered here, so the assertion should not be taken to rest solely on the modest evidence of the first paragraphs of *BGE*.

41. *Zarathustra* II, "On Self-Overcoming," in *Portable Nietzsche*, pp. 227. Also *BGE* 13, p. 211. Occasionally Kaufmann's excellent translation will be revised for the sake of greater literalness. Here we have only added Nietzsche's exclamation marks. The meaning of self-overcoming is also treated at, pp. 38–40, 60–65, and 94–95.

42. One could even say that the corrosive force of the doctrine of perspective is the principal cause of European decadence. "[T]he historical cycle of man-made, word-defining perspectives is the human expression of the essential nature of the Being-process (Becoming)—the will to power. When a given world perspective loses its capacity for self-concentration and self-transcendence, or what Nietzsche calls 'life-enhancement,' when its creative force is spent, the result is decadence. In the nineteenth century, European civilization is engaged in the death throes of a decadence characterized specifically by the sickness of historicism. Modern Europeans have realized that world perspectives are man-made, or transient and subjective." Stanley Rosen, *Nihilism: A Philosophical Essay* (New Haven, Conn.: Yale University Press, 1969), pp. 104–5.

43. See also note 20 above.

44. *Twilight*, "Maxims and Arrows," aph. 34, in *Portable Nietzsche*, p. 471. It is interesting at this point to recall Aristotle's reputation as the founder of the peripatetics. Cf. Plato, *Symposium* 174D–175B.

45. *Genealogy* I, 13, in *Basic Writings*, p. 481.

46. The classic-modern assertion seems largely operative in contemporary biology. Life is defined in the classroom and recognized in the laboratory as what metabolizes and/or reproduces, i.e., what nourishes itself and regenerates itself. The nature of the self that is regenerated is left in metaphysical darkness. One might say that the "genetic code" is the biological self—but how far does that really take us toward an answer, especially in view of conspicuous natural differences between "identical" twins with identical genetic codes?

47. *Zarathustra* II, "The Dancing Song," in *Portable Nietzsche*, pp. 220–21.

48. Ibid., "On Self-Overcoming," pp. 226–28. See Dannhauser, *Nietzsche's View of Socrates*, pp. 257–61, for an intelligent discussion of Life in *Zarathustra*.

49. The Stoics are called "noble" (*edel*, not *vornehm*). Perhaps Nietzsche intends this appellation as more than a mock compliment.

50. Dannhauser, *Nietzsche's View of Socrates*, p. 225. See also *Twilight of the Idols*, "'Reason' in Philosophy" and "How the 'True World' Finally Became a Fable."

51. *Twilight*, "Reason" in Philosophy" 2, in *Portable Nietzsche*, pp. 480–81.

52. That neural messages must be transferred to the spinal cord and brain before sense perception is possible can already suggest the impossibility of separating raw sensory information from interpretation. One could of course complain here that *this* point exactly *follows* Nietzsche rather than cutting athwart him, for who is more famous for asserting that man's world is a world of interpretation rather than text? We would insist, however, that the firm belief in the *fact* of becoming is at the core of Nietzsche's doctrines. Indeed, the teaching of the eternal return can be described as Nietzsche's effort to overcome the horrifying character of becoming without denying the fundamental fact of becoming.

53. *Twilight*, "The Problem of Socrates," in *Portable Nietzsche*, pp. 473–79. See note 26 above.

54. Kaufmann mistranslates *"sie würden hinaus wollen"* as "they would want to rise."

55. Uncharacteristically for this chapter, Nietzsche does not psychoanalyze Copernicus and Boscovich. He does, however, name their nationalities in a seemingly gratuitous fashion. Perhaps the suggestion is that the scientific doctrines of Copernicus and Boscovich were determined or colored by their homelands—but about this possibility we can only conjecture.

56. Strictly speaking, paragraph 12 alone is the central paragraph, but paragraphs 12 and 13 have such a strong link as to make them virtually inseparable. We cannot, incidently, attach much meaning to the particular numbers attached to paragraphs of Nietzsche's teachings, such as "9" and "13" to paragraphs on the will to power. The number "9" can be taken to indicate the Muses—this, be it remembered, is also the number of chapters in *Beyond Good and Evil*—and the number "13" is traditionally associated with chance and the occult. But we know of no evidence that Nietzsche intends these associations in numbering paragraphs as distinguished from chapters.

57. See, e.g., *Zarathustra* II, 12, "On Self-Overcoming," in *Portable Nietzsche*, pp. 225–28.

58. Harry Neumann, "Superman or Last Man?: Nietzsche's Interpretation of Athens and Jerusalem," *Nietzsche Studien*, V (1976), 1–28.

59. See paragraph 24, where Nietzsche expostulates against the concept of a *causa sui*.

60. See our discussion of paragraph 13, pp. 38–40 above.

61. It might be asserted that an omnipotent God would be causeless (cf. note 59 above). We would rejoin that an omnipotent God is unimaginable *qua* omnipotent, for an omnipotent God would have unimaginable powers, such as the power to create a multitude of other omnipotent Gods,

or the power to eliminate the possibility of there ever being or having been an omnipotent God. An omnipotent God would not be fettered by the principle of noncontradiction. Cf. note 67 below.

62. Nietzsche alludes to the famous remark of the French monarch, "I am the state." Just as Louis was in fact not the state, so is the will in fact not the effect.

63. *Nicomachean Ethics* 1139A-B. Aristotle's treatment of *proairesis* here is a little perplexing. He says that the beginning or first principle *(arche)* of doing is forechoice, and there cannot be forechoice without mind *(nous)* and thought *(dianoia)* or without a moral character trait *(ethikes hexeos)*. Since thinking itself moves nothing, forechoice must be appetitive mind or thinking appetite. Now Aristotle adds something apparently supererogatory, that such an *arche* is a human being. A human being is *proairesis*?

64. Cf. the first "nature" of paragraph 9, and our discussion of paragraph 4, at pp. 23–26 above.

65. A form of "nature" is used once each in paragraphs 11 and 12. In *BGE* 11 *natürlich* appears to be a casual expression — Kaufmann translates the German word as "of course" — but it may indicate that nature or the "in-itself" is the standard by which synthetic judgments a priori are judged false. In paragraph 12 "the soul" is lost when clumsy *(ungeschickte)* naturalists (cf. the clumsy philosophers of the preface to *BGE*) touch on it.

66. *"Twilight,"* "How the 'True World' Finally Became a Fable" 4–6, in *Portable Nietzsche*, pp. 485–86.

67. In *Zarathustra* II, "Upon the Blessed Isles," Zarathustra contends that the conjecture of God should not be allowed because conjectures should be limited by what is thinkable. But is the will to power, *pure* creativity, genuinely thinkable? *Portable Nietzsche*, p. 198.

68. Better, he effects this replacement in the entire corpus of his mature works. See also our discussion of paragraph 14, where the parallel between *BGE* 14 and 22 is considered.

69. *Twilight,* "Skirmishes of an Untimely Man" 45, in *Portable Nietzsche*, p. 549.

70. *Ibid.*, pp. 549–50. Compare especially Dostoevsky's *Notes from the Underground*. See also letters to Georg Brandes of October 20 and November 20, 1888, in Christopher Middleton, ed., *Selected Letters*, pp. 317, 327. It should be kept in mind that Nietzsche did not "discover" Dostoevsky until 1887, and thus is not *alluding* to him in paragraph 23. See letter to Franz Overbeck of February 23, 1887 in *Selected Letters*, pp. 260–61.

71. *Twilight,* "Skirmishes" 45, in *Portable Nietzsche*, pp. 549–51.

72. *The Antichrist* 31, in *Portable Nietzsche*, p. 603. Walter Kaufmann, *Nietzsche: Philosopher, Psychologist, Antichrist* (Princeton, N.J.: Princeton University Press), pp. 340–44.

73. *The Will to Power*, trans. Walter Kaufmann and R. J. Hollingdale and ed. Walter Kaufmann (New York: Vintage Books, 1967) 82, p. 51; 821, pp. 434–35.

74. See letter to Peter Gast of October 14, 1888, in Middleton, *Selected Letters*, p. 313; also *Basic Writings*, p. 587n8, and F. W. J. Hemmings, *The Russian Novel in France, 1884–1914* (New York: Oxford University Press, 1950), p. 241, cited in *Basic Writings*, p. 587n8.

75. The danger of overinterpretation is great, however. Thomas Mann plausibly suggested that the pale criminal in *Zarathustra* is Dostoevsky's Raskolnikov—but Nietzsche wrote *Zarathustra* years before ever reading a word of Dostoevsky. See Kaufmann, *Nietzsche*, p. 340n2.

76. Fyodor Dostoevsky, *Crime and Punishment*, trans. Constance Garnet (New York: Bantam Books, Inc., 1959), pp. 120, 176.

77. Ibid., p. 187. See *Twilight*, "Skirmishes," in *Portable Nietzsche*, p. 556. See also *BGE* 40, pp. 240–41.

78. E.g., ibid., pp. 396, 414.

79. Cf. *The Will to Power* 736, p. 390. Kaufmann mentions in his notes possible echoes of Dostoevsky in this and the preceding aphorism.

80. See Karl Lowith, *From Hegel to Nietzsche: The Revolution in Nineteenth Century Thought*, trans. David E. Green (Garden City, N.Y.: Doubleday and Co., Inc., Anchor Books, 1967), pp. 174–86. (One can of course have indirect debts that one does not duly appreciate.)

Hegel's critique of the subject-object distinction, which Nietzsche presupposes but never makes explicit, reappears in Heidegger (e.g., *Being and Time*, *Hegel and the Concept of Experience*). If the known is *absolutely* other than the knower, it is precisely *un*knowable, because there is by definition an unbridgeable gap between us and what is absolutely other; and if what is known is strictly object, the subject *qua subject* is unknowable. Thus the subject-object distinction purges the whole world of any possible knowledge.

Any serious challenge to Hegel's critique of subject-object would have to ask first, whether there is some slippage involved in Hegel's uses of the term "other," and second, whether Hegel perfectly succeeds in freeing his *own* discourse of the subject-object distinction.

81. *Zarathustra* I, "On the New Idol," in *Portable Nietzsche*, pp. 160–66.

82. See Eugen Fink, *Nietzsches Philosophie* (Stuttgart: Verlag W. Kohlhammer, 4th ed., 1979), pp. 74–82 and 91–100; Karl Löwith, *Nietzsche's Philosophy of the Eternal Recurrence of the Same*, trans. J. Harvey Lomax (Berkeley: University of California Press, 1997), pp. 88–94. See also ibid., p. 187: "Nietzsche, in recalling the pre-Socratic *physikoi*, engages in the great attempt to 'translate' man 'back' into the *nature* of all things; and because in metaphysics, which had become supraworldly and backworldly, he tries to gain acknowledgment again of the everlasting

physis of the world and the 'great reason of the body' as what is fundamental and exists always, remains the same and recurs."

83. *Zarathustra* I, "On the Three Metamorphoses," in *Portable Nietzsche*, pp. 137–39.

84. Ibid. Zarathustra defines "spirit" as "the life that itself cuts into
life: with its own agony it increases its own knowledge." And the spirit's
happiness is "to be anointed and through tears to be consecrated as a sacrificial animal." *Zarathustra* II, "On the Famous Wise Men," in *Portable
Nietzsche*, p. 216.

85. In *Zarathustra* the warriors of knowledge are the forerunners of
the saints of knowledge. To these warriors Zarathustra exclaims, "Your
love of life shall be love of your highest hope; and your highest hope shall
be the highest thought in life. Your highest thought, however, you should
receive as a command from me—and it is: man is something that shall be
overcome." I, "On War and Warriors," in *Portable Nietzsche*, p. 162. Are
the "warriors of knowledge" free spirits, and are the "saints of knowledge"
to which they are forerunners, philosophers of the future? If so, the free
spirits will be unfree in at least one respect, *viz.*, subordination to the will
of Nietzsche-Zarathustra. In that case the only *authentic* free spirit might
be Nietzsche-Zarathustra himself, or his like.

86. Nietzsche does not conceive the relationship as that between philosophy and politics per se. He seems to have a lower view of politics than
do the ancients. Insofar as religion implies politics, however, he can be
said to have a higher view.

87. Nietzsche's identification of himself with the free spirits and lack
of identification with the philosophers of the future may lead some readers to wonder whether the free lion might in important respects be superior to the creative child.

88. *Genealogy* III, 24 in *Basic Writings*, pp. 584–86.

89. Ibid., p. 586.

90. Ibid., p. 587.

91. Our interpretation of the next several paragraphs of *BGE* will
sometimes draw upon an unpublished and unapproved record of classroom lectures on Nietzsche by Leo Strauss at the University of Chicago
in 1967. As indicated in the preface, this book altogether profits from the
author's access to all three copyrighted transcripts of Strauss's courses on
Nietzsche of 1959, 1967, and 1971.

92. *Lysis* 212A. One could even say that the Nietzschean maxim "all
contact is bad contact except with one's equals" (*BGE* 26, p. 228) is a
brash but accurate statement of the heart of Aristotle's view of friendship
in the *Nicomachean Ethics*; after all, Nietzsche does admit that contact
with one's inferiors can be *useful*. Nevertheless, Aristotle might accuse
Nietzsche of fastidiousness.

93. Nietzsche speaks of Plato's "Sphinx-nature," perhaps recalling paragraph 1, where Nietzsche-Oedipus confronts the Sphinx. "Nature" occurs in some form only four times in the whole of chapter 2, and two of those occurrences are in paragraph 28. (Nature also occurs once each in paragraphs 26 and 36.) In paragraph 28 "nature" refers to the "character" of a man. Nietzsche seems to approve of both Lessing's "histrionic nature" (*Schauspieler-Natur*; cf. *BGE* 7) and Plato's "Sphinx-nature," even though Lessing falls short of Machiavelli's tempo and Plato is characterized as inferior to Aristophanes. Evidently a man's "nature" in this sense does not comprehend the whole man.

94. Zarathustra first presents the thought that the liberated will, free from the spirit of revenge, should will backwards, i.e., should will the eternal return. Thereupon the hunchback complains that Zarathustra speaks differently to different human types—one way to his pupils, another to hunchbacks, and still another to himself. The next speech is entitled "On Human Prudence." *Zarathustra* II, "On Redemption," in *Portable Nietzsche*, pp. 523–54. See Löwith, *Nietzsche's Philosophy of the Eternal Recurrence*, pp. xix–xxviii.

95. Nietzsche observes in *Twilight of the Idols* that in the sense of high culture, one is still a child at the age of thirty years. *Twilight*, "What the Germans Lack" 5, in *Portable Nietzsche*, p. 511.

96. Nietzsche might very well be referring to his own three stages of aesthetic romanticism, positivism, and Zarathustran maturity. See Lowith, *Nietzsche's Philosophy of the Eternal Recurrence*, pp. 21–26, and Dannhauser, *Nietzsche's View of Socrates*, pp. 19–20.

97. It seems that Nietzsche assumes that the alternative hypothesis, that will is fundamentally body, is absurd. But is the mystery from which strict materialism suffers any more insoluble than the mystery of Nietzsche's hypothesis?

98. *The Will to Power* 583C, p. 314. See Harry Neumann, "Superman or Last Man?," pp. 15–16.

99. See Strauss, "Note on the Plan," pp. 100–101. Here Nietzsche seems to presuppose that creation does require a creator after all. Cf. *BGE* 34 end, p. 237.

100. In this paragraph Nietzsche also speaks of "some who know how to muddle and abuse their own memory," i.e., those who devise a mask to hide their thoughts not from others but from themselves. *BGE* 40, p. 240. This aside anticipates a crucial paragraph in the chapter on nobility, *BGE* 278, pp. 413–14.

101. E.g., "Zarathustra's Prologue" 2, p. 124; 4, pp. 126–28; *Zarathustra* III, "The Convalescent" 3, p. 331.

102. At the end *Zarathustra* I, Zarathustra proclaims to his disciples that the gift-giving virtue is the highest virtue. Zarathustra also observes

that his disciples strive, as he does, for the gift-giving virtue. And here it does appear that his highest striving is for the gift of the superman. However, Zarathustra warns his disciples in this very discussion of gift-giving that he may be a deceiver. "On the Gift-Giving Virtue" 1–3, in *Portable Nietzsche*, pp. 186–91. Cf. *Ecce Homo*, Preface, 4, pp. 675–76.

103. See *Genealogy* III, 7, pp. 542–44; cf. Xenophon *Symposium* ii 10 and ix 7. Nietzsche's attachment to Lou Andreas-Salomé was apparently as much teacher-pupil as lover-beloved—in his letters he addressed her as "*Sie*" rather than "*Du*"—but one has to wonder whether Nietzsche over-rated her because of her attractiveness to him as a woman. See Kaufmann, *Nietzsche*, pp. 47–64; also Rudolph Binion, *Frau Lou: Nietzsche's Wayward Disciple* (Princeton: Princeton University Press, 1968). Finally, see letter to Franz Overbeck of September 9, 1882: "Das Nützlichste aber, was ich diesen Sommer getan habe, waren meine Gespräche mit Lou. *Unsre Intelligenzen* und Geschmacker sind im Tiefsten verwandt. . . ." (italics added): "The most useful thing I did this summer was [having] my conversations with Lou. Our intelligence and taste are most profoundly akin."

104. See Joseph Cropsey, *Plato's World* (Chicago: University of Chicago Press, 1995). Cf. Hans-Georg Gadamer, *The Idea of the Good in Platomic-Aristotelian Philosophy*, trans. P. Christopher Smith (New Haven, Conn.: Yale University Press, 1986), pp. 142–78.

105. *Birth of Tragedy* 13, in *Basic Writings*, pp. 88–89. Cf. *Twilight*, "The Problem of Socrates" 10–12, in *Portable Nietzsche*, pp. 478–79.

106. Concerning Nietzsche's idealization of Socrates, see Dannhauser, *Nietzsche's View*, especially pp. 87–102.

Chapter Three

The Eternal Recurrence and the Superman

> For me . . . the religious, that is, god-forming instinct now and then—sometimes at the wrong time—takes on life.
>
> —*The Will to Power* 1038[1]

Nietzsche's thematic treatment of religion in *Beyond Good and Evil* occurs in chapter 3, "The Religious Matter."[2] This discussion concludes the "theoretical" part of the text. We have seen that the first two chapters concern philosophy. Inasmuch as religion is the only other theoretical theme, one might be led to suppose that the theoretical part of the book pits philosophy against religion, or even Athens against Jerusalem. But by the end of chapter 2 Nietzsche has, as it were, annihilated philosophy in the traditional sense by stripping bare the moral faiths that masquerade as philosophic truths. Should any contest take place between traditional philosophy and religion, religion would win by default. As for the philosophers of the future, he locates them at the heart of Nietzschean religion in paragraph 56, where in a seeming paroxysm he promulgates the eternal return. In this light it would appear more accurate to say that Nietzsche assimilates philosophy and religion or transforms philosophy into religion.

This somewhat refined formulation of Nietzsche's intention will itself require substantial revision, however. Whereas *Thus Spoke Zarathustra* obviously revolves around the eternal recurrence and ends[3] with a series of spirited affirmations of eternity, in *BGE* there is only a single mention of the eternal recurrence. Nietzsche does not

recur to the eternal return even in the chapter on nobility. On the face
this manifest de-emphasis of the central teaching of the *Zarathustra*
is mysterious. But Nietzsche has already intimated the explanation
by taking care to distinguish himself from the philosophers of the future. He is the free spirit who does not believe in the religion of the
philosophers of the future. He is the promulgator of the eternal return who cannot himself will the eternal return.[4] Perhaps he is too
much a philosophic lover of truth, or rather of wisdom, simply to
abandon himself to the Nietzschean religious "truth" of the eternal
return? We suspect so. To be sure, he must mask his philosophic
reservations against the eternal recurrence in order to bring forth the
superman and therewith the religion of the future. But at the core of
Nietzsche's thought, the victory of religion over philosophy remains
highly imperfect.

The chapter on religion emphasizes the differences rather than the
similarities of various religions, for Nietzsche appears to believe that
there is no single heart of all religion.[5] Yet in contrast to the emphasized disparity and therewith irrationality of the subject matter taken
altogether, the plan of Nietzsche's treatment is lucid and coherent.
"Aphorisms 46–52 are devoted to religion hitherto and 53–57 to the
religion of the future. The rest of the chapter (aph. 58–62) transmits
Nietzsche's appraisal of religion as a whole. In the section on religion hitherto he speaks first of Christianity (48–48), then of the
Greeks (49), then again of Christianity (50–51), and finally of the
Old Testament (52)."[6] Paragraphs 58–60 concern the religious elevation of life, and paragraphs 61–62 consider the philosopher's effort to utilize religion for political purposes and the difficulties and
dangers of such an effort. And of course *BGE* 45 introduces the
"whole history of the soul so far [*BGE* 46–52] and its as yet unex-
hausted possibilities [*BGE* 53–57]" that Nietzsche sketches or adumbrates in this chapter. Were it not for Nietzsche's identification of
himself with Pascal, one might detect in Nietzsche's lucid and coherent treatment of religion in chapter 3 the scanning by an outsider,
a philosopher, of a foreign landscape. Even the impassioned an-
nouncement of the eternal recurrence (56) is followed immediately
by detached ridicule of the eternal recurrence (*BGE* 57), and on this
note the section on the religion of the future (53–57) ends.

Nietzsche begins the chapter on religion with the seemingly tau-
tologous observation that the human soul is the predetermined ob-

ject of study for a psychologist (*BGE* 45, p. 249). His suggestion here is by no means a tautology, however: for Nietzsche, what comprehends the heights, depths, and distances of inner human experience is, at least primarily, the history of religion. What warrant does he as psychologist have for emphasizing religion over, say, politics, or philosophy, or love? Formally speaking, we already know the answer: since fundamentally the human soul is the will to power, what comprehends inner human experience must be supremely expressive of that will. Religion, then, must be the fullest culmination of the will to power. This conclusion need not contradict the assertion that philosophy is the most spiritual will to power (*BGE* 9, p. 206); religion may be philosophy transformed, or philosophy may require a religious ideal for its perfection. Looking at Nietzsche's own basic philosophic doctrine, we can certainly say that the will to power requires the eternal recurrence for its perfection: the ultimate reducibility of everything to will remains incomplete until the entire universe is swept into and emerges out of the willing of the eternal return of the same. We might even go further and suggest that the doctrine of the will to power is asseverated *for the sake of* the eternal return, which the former requires for its perfection.[7] But to contend that Nietzschean philosophy requires a religious ideal for its perfection is not to affirm that Nietzsche is himself capable of subscribing to a religious ideal (cf. *BGE* 289).

Nietzsche complains in paragraph 45 that he must investigate the history of the human soul without a single helper. However nice it would be to have scholarly assistants to lighten his burden, he knows that scholars can never achieve understanding of religion, because they are *objective* men. Scholars see religion from the outside, but understanding of religion comes only from the inside, à la Pascal. Nietzsche must inquire alone because he alone is capable of seeing religions from the inside; evidently Nietzsche's conscience is as deep, as wounded, and as monstrous as Pascal's. To the extent that Nietzsche, or his persona, shares in Pascal's religiosity, he apparently shares in "a continual suicide of reason—a tough, long-lived, wormlike reason that cannot be killed all at once and with a single stroke" (*BGE* 46, p. 250).[8] However, even great religious figures such as Pascal can presumably see only a single religion from the inside—can Nietzsche see *every* religion from the inside, and at the same time all religions from above (*BGE* 45, p. 249)? It appears that

Nietzsche's demands upon the student of religion make a comprehensive view of religion, and therefore of the human soul, impossible. Thus he concludes the paragraph by calling his curiosity a vice and by indicating sarcastically that the love of truth is barren: "But a curiosity of my type remains after all the most agreeable of all vices—sorry, I wanted to say: the love of truth has its rewards in heaven and even on earth" (ibid., p. 250). Nevertheless, it is most likely that Nietzsche does consider himself more capable of putting religion into its proper light than any other mortal, presumably because Nietzschean religion is the highest religion, in terms of which all others should be understood. But must not a reliable judgment that his religion is the highest presuppose that, in the most crucial respect of all, religions altogether can be understood from the outside?

Nietzsche begins his sketch of the history of the human soul[9] by adverting to Christianity, to which he devotes much time in the chapter and away from which he never completely turns his attention. The religiosity of the Greeks and that of the Jews apparently are advanced primarily as counterpoints to Christianity, and even the eternal recurrence is described as the culmination of a sacrifice of God himself (*BGE* 55, p. 257). Why should "the" history of the human soul give such a huge emphasis to Christianity? In consideration of the vulgarity of Christianity, characterized by Nietzsche as a so-called religion of love that really stems from a vengeful spirit on the part of resentful losers against the winners and the world, it would seem unlikely that Christianity captures the peaks of the human soul. Perhaps the solution to the puzzle lies in the singularly political character of the chapter on religion within the theoretical part of the book? Through politics Christianity's revaluation of all values has indeed captured the human soul, at least the soul of man in the West. The most important fact for the historian of the human soul might be that the soul is now degraded in contrast to its earlier states and its potential state. Improvement of the soul requires above all overcoming Christianity and therewith a transformation of politics. The impotence of traditional philosophy to effect such improvement leads to the need for a more vigorous philosophy of the future to take charge of political life by means of religions for the multitudes (*BGE* 61, p. 262), presumably radically un-Christian religions. These political religions will be mere instruments of rule for the aristocracy and hence in Nietzsche's view will not be characterized by authentic religious life (*BGE* 58, p. 259; *BGE* 61, p. 263). The propounders of political life will be hypocrites, and the vulgar believers will of course be incapable of high spirituality. But the philosophy of the future will itself be a religion, an authentic religion that will satisfy the religious instinct of the aristocracy (*BGE* 53–57, pp. 256–59). The heart of the philosophy of the future develops out of a deep pessimism that is transcended by the will's willing the eternal recurrence, and that pessimism has Christian roots (*BGE* 56, p. 258; *BGE* 55, p. 257; *BGE* 46, pp. 250–51). For it is Christianity that teaches that, apart from the afterlife and the redemption of faith, the very essence of life on earth is senseless suffering. Perhaps the deepest reason for Nietzsche's emphasis on Christianity can be called the Christian origins of the eternal return?

Christianity is essentially a sacrificial religion, according to Nietzsche. Hence it is the early Christians rather than Luther or Cromwell who truly embody the Christian faith (*BGE* 46, p. 250). For faith offers the spirit not encouragement or consolation but the *absurdissimum*, the greatest *absurdity*. *Hitherto* there has never been such daring (*Kühnheit*) anywhere else as that to be found in the paradox of Christianity—in a formula, "God on the cross," the self-sacrifice of God—with the impressive result that Christianity has revalued all the values of antiquity. But the Christian revaluation of values is ignoble and reflects Oriental slavishness, in contradistinction to the noble (*vornehme*) and frivolous tolerance of Rome prior to the conquest of Rome by Christianity (ibid., pp. 250–51). Would it not be possible to revalue all prior values through affirming the great truth, the *absurdissimum*, of Christianity, without sinking into a slavish spirit of revenge? Nietzsche would like to suppose there is. Yet how can one both affirm like the Christians and deny like the aristocrats that life on earth is spent in a valley of tears?

This question gets its answer in the eternal recurrence. It merits repeating that the recurrence gets discussed only once, in paragraph 56, in *BGE*. The eternal recurrence is the final product of the thinking through of the meaning of pessimism. Prior to Nietzsche pessimism has never gotten beyond superficiality, not even in the case of Schopenhauer. Schopenhauer is a Christian and a German and therefore narrow and simple. Nietzsche, comprehensive and deep, recognizes that pessimism literally means what it says, that this is the worst of all possible worlds—and hence is an unbearable horror. Pessimism is nihilism. Once God has been cast off his throne, man must worship "the stone, stupidity, gravity, fate, the nothing" (*BGE* 55, p. 257). Nature supplies absolutely no guidance to man (cf. *BGE* 9, p. 205) and certainly no support for morality. Whereas nature is meaningless, human life is far worse than meaningless, because man is the only part of nature with the capacity to be tormented by the awareness of the nothing that guides and supports him. Best of all for human beings would be never to be, and second best is to die soon. Nietzsche is not exaggerating in the slightest when he claims that he has looked into "the most world-denying of all possible ways of thinking." Yet he claims that the result of this most profound nihilistic vision is the most resounding imaginable affirmation of the world. This high-hearted affirmation is the willing of the eternal recurrence of precisely that meaningless world that Nietzsche calls an abyss and a nothing. By willing that meaningless nature return to us in its full meaninglessness over and over eternally, Nietzsche renders the horrifying character of nature not only endurable but even inspiring. If one dances at the edge of an abyss, the abyss loses its fearsomeness. "Joy in tragedy" is the Dionysian formula for the eternal recurrence, and Dionysus solves the most profound human problem. What is amazing about the religiosity of the affirmer of the eternal return "is the enormous gratitude it exudes: it is a very noble type of human being that confronts nature and life in *this* way" (*BGE* 49, p. 254).

So it is the noble superman, the willer of the eternal return, who both affirms like the Christians and denies like the aristocrats that mortals live in a vale of tears. Grave questions remain. The gravest is, just how does the eternal recurrence render the horrifying character of meaningless nature inspiriting? For the moment we begin with a more superficial, albeit not unrelated, inquiry: Is not the doctrine of the eternal recurrence actually ignoble because of its Christian roots? We have seen that Nietzsche uses the formula "God on the cross" to indicate the essential meaning of Christianity. He explains this formula in *Antichrist* 51. In brief, all that suffers is divine; we sufferers, we, too, are divine. Nietzsche despises this sanctification of all that suffers. Yet as shown by Zarathustra's recurring horror at the ghastly thought of willing the endless return of all the human fragments and failures, in sanctifying all that was and is the eternal return, too, can be seen as sanctifying all that suffers. The role of this

horror in the drama of *Zarathustra* establishes at a minimum Nietzsche's awareness of the difficulty. How might he have addressed it?
There is some evidence that the eternal return implies not that all that
was and is, is divine, but rather that all that was and is, is the product of divinity. Nietzsche concludes *BGE* 56 with these queries:
"What? And would not this [the eternal recurrence, its affirmation,
or both] be *circulus vitosus deus?*" Presumably one cannot get
a world out of nothing without a god; this observation may explain
the absence of the word "nature" here. Taken anthropologically as
Nietzsche does here—in abstraction from the cosmological sense of
recurrence that refers, much as the ancients did, simply to the eternal
ebb and flow of self-consuming and self-replenishing nature—the
eternal return is not nature and not a product of nature. The return
originates in the will, in the divine will to power. Thus the doctrine
of eternal recurrence deifies not necessarily everything but perhaps
only the willer of the recurrence. Whereas the ignoble Christian formula is "all that suffers is divine," the noble Nietzschean formula
might be "only he who suffers most and redeems himself from his
own suffering is divine."

The comparison of the eternal return to Christianity has value
both for explaining the order of chapter 3 and for penetrating into
the meaning of the eternal return. It would be shocking, perhaps, but
nonetheless accurate, to observe that the doctrine of the eternal recurrence is Christianity for philosophers. The point is not just that
the recurrence begins with the Christian supposition that life on
earth exists in a valley of tears, and not just that the recurrrence incorporates the Christian exaltation of the deep sufferer who transcends his deep suffering. Given a certain twist, on these grounds
alone the eternal return might be said to follow Buddhism as much
as Christianity. But the connection to Christianity is much tighter,
for the self is not dissolved in Christianity as it is in Buddhism (see
Antichrist 20–23). Although Buddha endorses egoism, the critical
desideratum for Buddhism is the avoidance of pain by the ego. In
order to avoid pain, the ego must contract. Worst of all for the Bud-
dhist would be an excessive sensitivity. It is quite the contrary for
the Christian. In Christianity there is not a contraction but an ex-
pansion of the ego or self. Where the highest hopes of the idealized
Greek nobles would have been for the prosperity of their class or
community, the highest hopes of the Christians are for individual

bliss in the afterlife. This longing for blissful immortality for one's own self leads the Christian to renounce this life for the sake of the afterlife. The renunciation of this life occurs in the spirit of revenge. The doctrine of the eternal return adopts, in addition to what was mentioned previously, the glorification of the self and the spirit of revenge. For the eternal return is an expression of revulsion and hostility for meaningless nature, the nothing, the abyss, prior to the action of the will upon that meaningless nature. As it were, the superman gets even with nature for nature's inhospitality to man. Christianity is at the very heart of the eternal return. It is no coincidence that in the musical arrangement of chapter 3 of *BGE*, the eternal recurrence is the perfection of an earlier recurrent theme.

We are now in a position to unriddle the deepest perplexity in the eternal return. How does the willing of the eternal recurrence transform the horrifying pessimistic vision of nature? How does the recurrence emancipate the self from the insight into the purposelessness of human life and nature's inhospitality to man, and from worship of "the stone, stupidity, gravity, fate, the nothing"? If nature is willed to repeat its cycle infinite times, so that man experiences the meaningless of nature infinite times, what sense does it make to say that man has been in any way emancipated? On the contrary, does the eternal return not enslave man to the worst possible extent? The repetition of madness does not constitute sanity, and would seem to provide no basis for establishing sanity. The eternal return seems to accomplish only one thing for the self. That one thing is just what the Christian dispensation offers, namely to guarantee that the self will never perish. The man who wills the eternal return wills the extirpation of the thought of his own mortality. With respect to death he makes himself a god. Some abysmal arrogance seemingly inspires Nietzsche with the insane hope that because he knows how to tyrannize himself, nature, too, lets herself be tyrannized.

Zarathustra would, if confined to prose, object to the above as follows. Willing of the eternal recurrence expunges the spirit of revenge through and through: it converts all that was and is from accident and riddle imposed by an external (and internal) fate beyond human control into the object of human desire (*wollen*). I will never resent anything again, since everything exists as it is because I willed it so. Instead of seething over the harshness or injustice of fate, I become a lover of fate. I embrace the whole of the world for all eternity, and can exclaim, I love you eternity! Thus with one stroke I satisfy the deepest erotic desire and become completely at home in the world and well pleased with my lot. The willing of the eternal recurrence accordingly brings the greatest reconciliation, relief, joy, and celebration. The man who wills in this superhuman mode achieves the perfect transcendence of nihilism. He both experiences the highest joy and bears the most serious responsibility, for now he lives as he must live again in all eternity.[10] Hence the superman is the peak and ultimate meaning of all human existence.

Socrates would find the Zarathustran self-defense both implausible and superficial. Two simple Socratic questions move like daggers to the heart of the matter: Does the sheer willing of something make it good? Obviously not, as common experience illustrates a trillion times over. Does the sheer willing of something make it true? Obviously not, as common experience illustrates a trillion times over. Among other things, Zarathustra abstracts from the problem of error. The protective walls of rhetoric around the eternal recurrence already begin to crumble beyond repair upon the enemy's first sally.

We return to the issue of death. If the eternal return were a fact, if Nietzsche's corporealist doctrine of the immortality of the soul were a knowable truth, man might be untroubled in the face of death. However, in *BGE* Nietzsche does not present the eternal return as factual. Quite the opposite—it must be willed with such passion that the willer of the eternal return unreservedly believes in it. The "truth" about the world is absolutely dependent upon will, consonant with the doctrine of the will to power. That doctrine can serve a moral purpose for the profound man who, pained by insight into nature's inhospitality toward man, wishes to live in a world sufficiently friendly to man to allow him somehow to survive. The profound man can fulfill his wish only by abolishing nature. The doctrine of the will to power does so by replacing nature with will. The willer becomes a creator, and his creation par excellence is the eternal recurrence. But how can the willer, however strong his passions, believe in the eternal return if he knows it not to be a fact? Apparently, in the "Seven Seals" of *Thus Spoke Zarathustra*, through the strength of his own affirmation Zarathustra does come to believe in the recurrence. But Zarathustra is not a real human being. And especially considering the concluding speech, it has to be said that

Zarathustra's development in the first three parts of the *Zarathustra* resembles a continual suicide of reason, "a tough, long-lived, wormlike reason that cannot be killed all at once and with a single stroke." Nietzsche's towering intelligence makes it virtually inconceivable that he overlooked either the Christian roots of the eternalization of the self or the necessity, in order for that project to succeed, of sacrificing something very high in man.

Immediately after the presentation of the eternal return, as we have noticed, Nietzsche compares his doctrine to a child's toy and a child's pain. The toys and pains of childhoood are transcended; the eternal return, too, must be transcended. Once one sees a child's toy and pain for what they are, once one recognizes that the eternal return must be transcended, one's understanding is superior to that of the affirmer of the return. But the affirming believer in the eternal return is Zarathustra: how can Nietzsche be superior to his own ideal? We are compelled to reexamine the relationship of Zarathustra to *BGE*. We recall that in *Ecce Homo* Nietzsche compares *Thus Spoke Zarathustra* to the first six days of creation and *BGE* to the seventh day. In the eyes of one who believes that the peak of humanity is the most creative self, that peak occurs in the *Zarathustra*. The *Zarathustra* is thus far superior to *BGE*. But whereas God created the world on the first six days, on the seventh day He did more than rest. On that day He looked around and saw what He had done. The seventh day was the day of contemplation. Whereas the *Zarathustra* is Nietzsche's creative work par excellence, *BGE* is his contemplative work par excellence. From the viewpoint of philosophy, then, the seventh day is superior to the six days of creation, *BGE* is superior to the *Zarathustra*. One who takes Nietzsche at his word studies *BGE* with such care because it is the best commentary on the *Zarathustra*. To the extent that Nietzsche the philosopher is superior to Zarathustra the believer, however, *Beyond Good and Evil* is Nietzsche's most profound work.

Paragraph 57 of *BGE* is understandably brief—Nietzsche does not want to call too much attention to his reservations against the eternal recurrence. As we have noted, the recurrence is supposed to make life worth living. For example, without the eternal return, the profound man's awareness that he will soon die can be devastating. The profound man "knows" that he will die because he knows that he is body. What is composed of connected bits of matter will eventually disintegrate into disconnected bits of matter. Thus one could say that corporealism contributes to the moral requirement for the doctrines of the will to power and the eternal return. One could add that the failure of Nietzsche's project results in part from the resistance of corporealism to complete assimilation into those doctrines, i.e., that Nietzsche is not totally convinced that "to be" means "to will and be willed" rather than "to have extension." Whether life is worth living seems to have a close tie to questions of what and why things are. We shall confine ourselves here to a brief examination of four possible answers: corporealism, "Platonic ideas," divine will, and the will to power.

According to the corporealist, all the things that are, are composed of body. Each thing that man experiences through his senses is what it is because of aggregations of little bits and separations of little bits. The first mystery is why the bits or atoms aggregate at all. Lucretius answers as adroitly as anyone can: the atoms have hooks that latch onto one another as they drift through space. But why are there atoms and not nothing? The atoms are eternal. Out of something something comes, and out of nothing nothing comes. What is must be, and must be always. We know that body is, because we experience bodies through our senses, and we know that the atoms are, because we see with our eyes that larger bodies are composed of smaller bodies that in turn are composed of smaller bodies, and smaller bodies of still smaller bodies. For the corporealist it follows that the atom, the cell of Being, is and must be eternally. As for the meaning of body, it evidently is identical with extension. Anything that is has length, width, and depth.

Corporealism is exposed to at least four complaints. Length, width, and depth are relations; do they not require a relator to do the relating? Can the corporealist prove that space and time are not simply built into the human mind, can he prove that they exist in the world in itself? Far from following the ineluctable dictate of experience, is not corporealism a mere hypothesis? Second, what is the status of truth for corporealism? Corporealism is of interest only if its exponent claims to know the truth about the world. But if corporealism is true, everything that is can be located in space. Where, then, is the space that truth occupies? Since truth is not corporeal, by strict corporealist doctrine there is no truth. Third, how can mere extension think? Even if the movements of particles are necessary for thinking to occur, it is difficult to see what could warrant calling those movements thinking. Finally, to shift to a moral objection, in equalizing everything, corporealism is ignoble.

With misgivings about our competence, we turn to the so-called Platonic ideas. Before recounting the general doctrine, we must recall that consideration of unresolved paradoxes and unanswered objections dominates the principal Platonic and Aristotelian discussions of the ideas. Furthermore, significant discrepancies arise within the Platonic dialogues between the accounts offered by Parmenides, the mature Socrates, and the Eleatic Stranger. At any rate, by this version of Being, to be means to be intelligible. The things that most truly are, are the eternal ideas. The transient, empirical things occur not in the world of Being but in the world of becoming. Yet the things of experience do participate in the ideas, for the form of a thing is in a sense its cause. Of which things there can be ideas is not altogether clear. In the *Republic*, for example, Socrates speaks of ideas of bigger and smaller (369a), the good (380d-e, 505a, 507b, 508e, 517c), the beautiful itself (479a), the fair itself (507b), light (507e), a regime (544c), a couch and a table (596b), and implements (ibid.). He also makes sweeping mention of the idea of each thing that is (486d) and the ideas of all things that are many (507b). However, in the *Parmenides* the young Socrates denies that there can be ideas of the lowest and pettiest things (130c). There is no question, though, about which of the ideas is supreme: the idea of the good. It provides the truth to the things known and gives to the knower the power to know. Employing "the idea of the good" and "the good" synonomously, Socrates asserts that the good is not being but is beyond being. The idea of the good is the object of the greatest study, for through it just things and other things become useful and beneficial (505a). Supreme in the intelligible realm, the idea of the good is more powerful and has higher dignity than being (508e). Like the other ideas, the idea of the good is eternal.

Of the conceivable grounds for finding the "Platonic ideas" unsatisfactory, four deserve our attention here. First is the relational problem of the referents of the ideas, the problem reflected in the aforementioned contradictory accounts in *Parmenides* 130c and *Republic* 486d and 507b. Either an infinitely expandable or an arbitrarily restricted number of ideas would seem to jeopardize the intelligibility of the ideal realm. The spokesman for the doctrine as presented not only fails to specify a rationally defensible basis for limiting the number of ideas, but stumbles over precisely this issue. Second, "Platonism" in its way undermines the status of truth. Truth as pure intelligibility is radically separated from the empirical world, that world in which humanity most emphatically finds itself. Third, just as the advocates of corporealism cannot show how body can think, so do the Platonic spokesmen for idealism fail to explain what it means for things to participate in the ideas. Finally, if Glaucon is right to suspect that the Platonic good is pleasure (509a), that hedonistic doctrine can pose a threat to nobility. If, on the other hand, at this point Socrates tells Glaucon to avoid blaspheming (ibid.) because the Platonic good is a universal God of all and a prefiguration of the Christian deity, Nietzsche has a strong case for accusing Plato-Socrates of laying the groundwork for the slave revolt in morals.

Divine creationism offers another answer to the question of Being. God brings the universe into being out of nothing through an act of will. What exists, God created, and what God has not created does not exist. Divine creation is possible because divinity inherently has miraculous powers that exceed human understanding. If one asks about the cause of the divine, the "theologians" will answer that God is eternal.

The divine-creationist dispensation on what it means to be is subject to the following criticisms. If Being is in relation to divinity, Being depends upon divine action. But God is a perfect being. What is perfect needs nothing. What needs nothing, wants nothing, and what wants nothing, does nothing out of will or desire. Theology in the strict sense, the logos of divinity that is adumbrated late in the second book of Plato's *Republic*, tells us that all divine actions, including divine creation, are impossible. From the point of view of revelation, though, this complaint amounts to a rationalistic quibble. A second, much graver objection against divine creation as an explanation of Being is that creationism undermines truth. Accepting divine creationism amounts to rejection of the principle of noncontradiction as a vehicle for arriving at truth, for Being itself is contradictory if it emerges out of nothing. Contradiction occupies the very core of the world. Otherwise put, divine creationism eliminates nature as a standard or measure. It goes without saying that creationism does offer an alternative to the truths of philosophy, namely the divine truths accessible through prophecy or revelation. But the multitude of conflicting prophecies and contradictory claims about divine revelation make it impossible to rely on prophecy or revelation per se unless we have a reliable means of sorting the chaff from the wheat. How can we identify the one true prophet among the many false ones? Here reason proves altogether impotent, for reason depends on the principle of noncontradiction, whereas divine revelation claims to transcend that principle. No miracle, no willed contradiction, exceeds the capacity of God in his omnipotence. Even if one directly experiences what seems a direct revelation from the divine, how can one know that what seems to be a revelation is truly one? Strong passions also do not adequately attest to religious truth, as the fervor with which incompatible messages are avowed makes clear. Third, how can supernature act upon nature? Through "miracles," yes, but what on earth does that term mean? If "miracle" means "something I do not understand and of which I cannot begin to provide any intelligible account," it would seem more candid simply to state one's ignorance than to presume to offer an impressive explanation of the world. Fourth, from Nietzsche's point of view, permanent subjugation to the yoke of an omnipotent God's will infuses the psyche with a repulsive slavishness, just as the focus on the afterlife leads, or amounts, to nihilism.

Whatever the cosmology of divine creation may do to truth and to nature, however, certain it is that nobility and religious faith "naturally" have much in common. Perhaps no one has launched a harsher attack against Scriptural religion—primarily Christianity—than Nietzsche has, but even he recognizes the loftiness of the teaching that man's lovableness derives from his having been made in the image of God. "To love man *for God's sake*—that has been the noblest and most remote feeling attained among men. That the love of man is just one more stupidity and brutishness if there is no ulterior intent to sanctify it; that the inclination to such love of man must receive its measure . . . from some higher inclination—whoever . . . first felt and 'experienced' this, . . . let him remain holy and venerable for us for all time as the human being who has flown highest yet and gone astray most beautifully!" (*BGE* 60, p. 262). One might even go so far as to say that nobility requires divinity; if the superman is noble, he is also divine (*BGE* 55–56, pp. 257–58, and *BGE* 150, p. 280).

The doctrine of the will to power also advances an account of why there are things and not nothing. We call it the fourth option with some uncertainty, for it is not altogether clear that the doctrine of the will to power does not collapse into an eccentric version of divine creationism. In any case, the doctrine holds that the Being of all things derives from will. The identity of the willer is left cloudy in Nietzsche's various accounts of the will to power. Sometimes it seems as though the world altogether or the individual things do the willing, and sometimes it seems that the will operates without any willer at all. Taken anthropologically, i.e., following the main thrust of *Thus Spoke Zarathustra* and *BGE*, the willer of the will to power is the superman who wills the eternal recurrence of the same. Despite these discrepancies regarding the willer, one thing is certain, namely that the will to power and the eternal recurrence are eternal. The eternity of the will is part and parcel of the eternity of the eternal return. But in the *Zarathustra* and *BGE* the eternal return is eternal because it is willed so by the most noble human being. Thus the doctrine of the will to power presents us with a never-never world in which a chimera is the Belly of Being—Dionysus in front, the Scriptural God behind, and Zarathustra in the center.

Apart from the difficulties already identified, the teaching of will to power gives rise to the following objections. First, as Nietzsche describes it, all willing is relational. He remarks in *BGE* 19: "In all willing there is, first, a plurality of sensations, namely, the sensation of the state '*away from which*,' the sensation of the state '*towards which*,' the sensations of this '*from*' and '*towards*' themselves, and then also an accompanying muscular sensation that, even without our putting into motion 'arms and legs,' begins its action by force of habit as soon as we 'will' anything." In the same paragraph he contends that "the will is not only a complex of feeling and thinking, but it is above all an affect, and specifically the *affect* of command. What is termed 'freedom of the will' is essentially the affect of superiority in relation to him who must obey." If willing is a relation between commander and obeyer, must not the commander and the obeyer exist by nature rather than by will? It seems that the doctrine of the will to power cannot fulfill the promise to give a comprehensive account of all things. The second objection against the doctrine is that it contradicts itself. Here we echo the hackneyed yet valid complaint against the truth that there is no truth. Nietzsche anticipated this objection and might retort that the truths of poetry and music are higher and profounder than dialectical truths; only by transcending the principle of noncontradiction can man penetrate to the Belly of being. If rationality is human, the passions of Zarathustra are divine. But with reason discredited and nought but passion to guide us, how can we distinguish between ascension into the divine and degeneration into the subhuman? Third, how does the will act upon the things? Nietzsche tries to avoid a dualism by calling everything will to power. In that case the will to power is dumb and stupid and ultimately purposeless, for the power to be increased and discharged has no goal beyond itself. The will to power in this "cosmological" sense is indistinguishable from sheer, universal becoming. But Nietzsche does not by any means rest content with this account. As we have just seen, the anthropological distinction between commander and commanded remains. So what is the interface between the two, and how does it function? Nietzsche no more answers this question than do the corporealists, idealists, and divine creationists resolve the parallel dualistic difficulties in their systems. Fourth, as becomes explicit in *The Genealogy of Morals*, the doctrine of the will to power has the moral consequence that all is permitted or that might makes right. Even if one conceded that the blond beasts of which Nietzsche speaks might display a crude sort of nobility, obviously a large number of mighty victors in many political orders past and present lack nobility and scarcely inspire moral admiration by the well-informed. Zarathustra would evidently prefer to say not "all is permitted" but "only that is choiceworthy which contributes to the coming of the superman." The superman is the superhuman being who develops out of man but transcends him, the being whose nobility is identical with his self-conquest or self-overcoming. In this sense the superman perfects the will to power by tying man back into nature, which equals becoming, which equals self-overcoming, which equals will to power. The superman is also the supreme warrior, because he gains his victory over himself, he overcomes himself. The grandest self-conquest is transcendence of the self's horizons. Recognizing the horizonal character of his own values, the superman destroys those values and then creates new values, only to destroy them and begin again. Warfare thus spiritualized glorifies the soul and makes it noble. But if all horizons are destined for destruction, must not even the horizon under which warfare is glorious be replaced? Neither an affirmative nor a negative answer can transcend the internal contradiction. Perhaps Nietzsche would reply "yes" (see *BGE* 296, pp. 426–27). Zarathustra responds by treating as sacred the horizon of the superman in which spiritual warfare is glorious and the outcome of willing is the eternal recurrence. This new religion of superman and eternal recurrence partakes of the same theoretical difficulties found in more traditional doctrines of revelation, however. And the egalitarian tendencies of "universal will to power" and "all is permitted" do not dovetail with any conception of warrior nobility, particularly not the spiritual one promoted by Zarathustra.

All four of these diverse accounts of Being—in terms of body, of Platonic ideas, of divine will, and of will to power—recur to eternity to explain why there is something rather than nothing. Is it the nature of the question that one must appeal to eternity for an answer? Or does the appeal to eternity not rather amount to an evasion of the question, to which a forthright response would be an admission of ignorance and a spirit of wonder? In recurring to eternity, does metaphysics, including the Nietzschean metaphysics of will to power and eternal recurrence, strive to rest satisfied with ultimately unphilosophic dogmas?[11] Or, on the contrary, does the effort to expunge eternity result in a replacement of eternal *physis* by convention or fantasy? Wherever these questions might eventually take us, Heidegger is unquestionably right to observe that under rigorous scrutiny the most famous treatments of Being leave us with more questions than answers. Much, and not least the hidden teaching of Plato's *Sophist*,[12] speaks in favor of Heidegger's recommendation that we approach the question of Being anew by ceasing to regard Being as a thing.

Our ignorance about Being would seem to make all our reflections highly tentative. Nevertheless, we must return to the issue that led us into the question of Being. That issue is the horrible character of the thought of the mortality—not apodictically demonstrated—of the self. According to Zarathustra, the courage of the affirmer of the eternal recurrence serves to conquer this thought: "Courage . . . slays even death itself, for it says, 'Was that life? Well then! Once more!'" (*Thus Spoke Zarathustra* III, "On the Vision and the Riddle" 1). In an aphoristic trilogy in the chapter on nobility in *BGE* (277–79, pp. 413–14),

Nietzsche indicates just how deeply a noble soul can suffer over awareness of its mortality. First he introduces the topic with a strange riddle that bewails the finality of the past and hence of time: "Bad enough! The same old story! When one has finished building one's house, one suddenly realizes that in the process one has learned something one needed to know in the worst way—before one began. The eternal distasteful 'too late!' The melancholy of everything *finished*!" (*BGE* 277, p. 413). The "eternal distasteful 'too late'" replaces the eternal recurrence of the same; for the most noble man, for Nietzsche himself perhaps, the eternal recurrence will not solve the problem of the finality of time and hence of death. Once a profound man has knowledge of the ugliness of death and of nature's inhospitality to man, it is too late to turn back, and the knower must pay a high price in suffering.

> Wanderer, who are you? I see you walking on your way without
> scorn, without love, with unfathomable eyes; moist and sad like a
> a sounding lead that has returned to the light, unsated, from every
> depth—what did it seek down there?—with a breast that does not
> sigh, with a lip that conceals its disgust, with a hand that now reaches
> only slowly: Who are you? What have you done? Rest here: This
> spot is hospitable to all—recuperate! And whoever you may be:
> What do you like now? What do you need for recreation? Name it:
> Whatever I have I offer to you!
> 'Recreation? Recreation? You are inquisitive! What are you
> saying?! But give me, please ———'
> What? What? Say it!
> 'Another mask! A second mask!' [*BGE* 278, pp. 413–14].

Nietzsche himself is, of course, the Wanderer. He does not tell us what the second mask is; he masks its identity. But he does elaborate the meaning of the first mask: It is what conceals, and is needed to conceal, the philosopher's thought from other men. The second mask, then, the source of relief for which the Wanderer desperately longs, is the mask of the philosopher's thought from himself. Why does Nietzsche need the second mask? "Men of profound sadness betray themselves when they are happy: They have a way of embracing happiness as if they wanted to crush and suffocate it, from jealousy; Alas, they know only too well that it will flee" (*BGE* 279, p. 414) If we are not dealing with a yet another mask of him here, Nietzsche wishes to mask from himself the transitory character of his own noble existence. He might prefer to believe that there is no truth rather than to live with the truth he knows, "for truth is ugly" (*The Will to Power* 598). Could one reason for his esotericism be to protect even his best readers from understanding him? "Every profound thinker is more afraid of being understood than of being misunderstood. The latter may hurt his vanity, but the former his heart, his sympathy, which always says: Alas, why do you want to have as hard a time as I did?'" (*BGE* 290, p. 419). Life is short, and when it ends man loses everything: "Nietzsche draws our attention to the paramountcy of being-oneself, of being for oneself, of 'preserving' oneself" (Strauss, "Note on the Plan," p. 104). Most important for man is his passionate attachment to himself and to his here-and-now. But the here-and-now, man's world, is poised to exterminate him in the next instant, and the depth of man's passionate nature serves to prepare for man's deep suffering if he discovers his fate. Thoroughgoing *amor fati* would require faith in the eternal recurrence of the same.

Socrates, the man of courage who faces death without the solace of religion, would likely disapprove of the supposition that death is quite such a horror and of the resulting sentimentality. The Nietzsche of *Twilight of the Idols* would dismiss the bravado of Socrates the suicidal nihilist: for Socrates life is no good, so death is a relief ("The Problem of Socrates" 12). Two other possible explanations for Socrates' equanimity before death deserve consideration, however. First, Socrates is famous for relating tales of the immortality of the soul. Yet the myths he offers are contradictory, and typically he even presents them as myths, as in the case of the myth of Ur. Moreover, in Plato's *Apology* Socrates acknowledges his complete ignorance about the afterlife and considers the possibility that death means complete annihilation. So it seems highly unlikely that these myths offer him much comfort. A more serious means of explaining his mastery of his passions even in the face of death derives from his understanding not of the afterlife but of himself and his humanity. Evidently Socrates regards the soul governed by the developed rational faculty as highest, best, and most distinctively human. When active, the developed reason is in large part hardly distinguishable from the questions or truths apprehended. If these questions or truths transcend time, so in a sense does what is most emphatically Socratic. If not, Socrates can nevertheless continue his

essential intellectual activity beyond his death by liberating other
potential Socratics from the conventions that enslave them. His selfishness leads to his philanthropy, and his philanthropy so to speak
slays death.

Nietzsche might respond by attacking the status of the ideas, possibly setting off a dialogue on the ideas and the will to power along
the lines sketched above. But Socrates could reply that it suffices
for him if certain fundamental questions survive, that otherwise
nothing critical depends on the status of the ideas. An alternative
Nietzschean objection to Socrates's view of death might also merit
attention. Nietzsche would ask Socrates, do you not philosophize in
order to secure a sense of strength or of pleasure? It is not clear that
in all candor Socrates could candidly answer in the negative, though
he would prefer to speak of the goal as a good and happy life. Affirmation would elicit another question. Is it, Nietzsche would press
Socrates, the rational faculty alone or even primarily that experiences the sense of strength or pleasure you lust after? To speak the
truth, Socrates might have to say "no." Then, Socrates, you philosophize for the sake of your transitory self, not some abstract faculty? So what is good, good for you, is destined for utter destruction
in the blink of an eye? Conceivably Socrates could maintain that
philosophizing is not only good for the self of the individual
philosopher, but also good in itself. A sign of this intrinsic goodness
could be said to be the admiration that one philosophic nature will
immediately have for another philosophic nature from which, because of circumstances, the former has nothing to gain. Be all the
foregoing as it may, Socrates and Nietzsche concur only once on
which traits should belong to the cardinal virtues: the two geniuses
agree only that courage is a mode of human excellence. (Cf. *BGE*
284 and *Dawn* 556 with *Republic* 427e, 395c.)

Once one has concluded the discussion of the doctrines of the will
to power and the eternal recurrence of the same with the noble superman and philosopher of the future in view, one's primary work
with Nietzsche is, as it were, complete. In *BGE*, after Nietzsche has
addressed the central doctrine of the religion of the future, what remains is to educate man in the direction of the superman who will
orient his life and all of politics toward that religion. This educational project is the principal subject of the rest of *BGE* after chapter
4, although at the end of the book Nietzsche seems to despair of his

educational project and to enter into beautiful laments, dialogues, and reveries. In speaking in this general way of the development of *BGE*, we seem to insist on a strong continuity within the book, the continuity of a moral tour de force that begins with the first word and is never lost sight of. Thus, we seem to contradict our earlier conjecture that the lack of order in chapter 4 is intended to point to a discontinuity between the theoretical and practical parts of *BGE*. But we continue to believe that Nietzsche's doctrine of nobility does not follow necessarily from the doctrine of the will to power. The doctrine of the will to power does not in strictest logic require the coming of the superman, but only prepares the way for him—*or* for a hastening of the development and spread of his disgusting antipode, the last man. With the doctrine of the eternal return and the superman Nietzsche attempts to forge a new moral order out of the doctrine of the will to power; but the likely lesson of chapter 4 is that we should suspect ourselves as interpreters whenever we impose order upon what is "by nature" chaotic.

We return briefly to chapter 3. Christianity has so corrupted man that it is as if a single malicious will dominated Europe for eighteen centuries in order to bring about the degeneration and atrophy of humanity. To expunge the pusillaninimity of nineteenth-century man, to overcome the greatest obstacle to the superman, Nietzsche must devote his energies to a denunciation of Christianity (*BGE* 62, pp. 264–66). In contrast to Christianity the religiosities of the Greeks and the Jews are described as noble and grand (*BGE* 49, p. 254, *BGE* 52, pp. 255–56). The Christian religion, which both draws upon and fosters slavish ecstasies, is the legacy of the rabble (*BGE* 49 and 50, p. 254).

Nevertheless, the Christian man par excellence, the saint, has prompted "the most powerful human beings" to bow reverentially before him (*BGE* 51, p. 255, *BGE* 47, pp. 251–52). The saint is awesome because of the sacrifices he makes; among other things he sacrifices food, sexual activity, and the company of other men. These sacrifices are all the more remarkable because often there is first an "extravagant voluptousness" that is then transformed into what seems to be a radical denial of the world and of the will. Nietzsche does not find this sequence astonishing, because he denies that a succession of opposites occurs: there is no "bad man" who suddenly turns into a "good man." Rather, the phenomenon of the saint manifests the dominion of the will to power in man's soul. The ruling element of the soul can be likened to Cesare Borgia, and the voluptousness of the "bad man" can be compared to the rampages of Remirro de Orca in Machiavelli's *Prince* (7). Both the performance of excesses and the ruthless extermination of the performer thereof are dictated by the prince for the sake of his unchallenged dominion. The will to power is the prince of the soul, a far more daring prince than even Cesare Borgia. The "most powerful human beings" sense something of this daring in the saint: "they sensed the superior force that sought to test itself in . . . conquest, the strength of the will in which they recognized and honored their own strength and delight and dominion: They honored something in themselves when they honored the saint. Moreover, the sight of the saint awakened the suspicion in them: Such an enormity of denial, of anti-nature will not have been desired for nothing, they said to and asked themselves. There may be a reason for it, some very great danger about which the ascetic, thanks to his secret comforters and visitors, might have inside information. . . . They had to ask him———" (*BGE* 51, p. 255). They had to ask him, presumably, what great calamity he seeks to escape, what higher rapture he enjoys. Nietzsche answers this question with ease in *BGE* and *The Genealogy of Morals*. The fear is the fear of nihilism, of the meaninglessness of the suffering of this world. The joy is the delight in cruelty. The cruel man's delight surges when he celebrates the exercise of his godlike powers over his victim, and the sublimest delight obtains from cruelty against one's own strongest instincts (*BGE* 55, p. 257). So the saint is the precursor of the superman. The saint's otherworldliness, however, limits his nobility. The superman is the saint ennobled.

As previously noted, paragraphs 58–60 treat the religious elevation of life and 61–62 consider the philosopher's effort to use religion for political purposes and the difficulties and dangers of such an effort. These passages show that in spite of his extremism, Nietzsche is quite capable of fair-mindedness and levelheadedness. The concluding observations in chapter 3 about the relationship between philosophy and religion probably constitute his closest approach in *BGE* to the practical wisdom of Plato and Aristotle. Nietzsche grants that a genuinely religious life is ennobling in its leisurely self-examination and prayerful disposition. He condemns the modern scholars and so-called free spirits who stupidly look down upon religion as a vestige of the dark ages. These self-supposed enlightened and emancipated ones Nietzsche castigates as presumptuous dwarfs and rabble. In contradistinction to modernity and especially modern science, religion has in important cases lifted man into a higher spirituality. Religion at its best has attempted to impose upon the democratic instincts a reverence for the high and the holy. At best prayerful solitude and the contemplative reverence of the Sabbath divert men from frenzied and small-minded business and hence from their longing for the green-pasture happiness of the herd. At a minimum, community prayer requires the rabble to be quiet and keep still for a change. "[T]hat way they become more beautiful for a while and—look more like human beings" (*The Gay Science* 128). Nietzsche even goes so far as to say that prior to him piety may have been the most powerful artistic device for beautifying man (*BGE* 59, p. 261). And as we have seen, the noblest man so far may have been the one who first loved man for the sake of God (*BGE* 60, p. 262).

Like the ancients, Nietzsche wishes to subordinate religion to philosophy in politics. The philosopher of the future will be responsible for the development of all humanity, and he will find religion a very useful educational instrument. Religion has special utility for teaching the many subjects to obey the few rulers. Nietzsche speaks of this education as a "betrayal" of the subjects. But far from spurning religion as the opiate of the masses, he in effect endorses it, when judiciously applied by the philosopher of the future, as a noble lie. Only through religion can the proper ordering of the great politics of the future come about. The exalted religious functions of the supreme men, the philosophers/priests/poets of the future, will allow them to escape from the day-to-day business of politics. Like the Brahmins, this higher caste of men will appoint the political leaders and then withdraw to their preferred life of contemplation and writing. As for the rulers who do immerse themselves in "the *necessary* dirt of politics," religion will prepare them for rule by making demands of asceticism and puritanism. "Asceticism and puritanism are almost indispensable means for educating and ennobling a race that wishes to become master over its origins and that works its way up toward future rule" (*BGE* 61, pp. 262–63). To the herd, to those who exist only to serve their superiors, religion gives contentment and fulfillment through divine sanctification of their work. This function has a direct parallel in the noble lie of Plato's *Republic*, the autochthonist tall tale that Socrates recommends to provide a divine origin and purpose for the system of classes and the class-based division of labor. Nietzsche admits that Christianity, too, serves this function of "teaching even the lowliest how to place themselves through piety into an illusory higher order of things and thus to maintain their contentment with the real order, in which their life is hard enough—and precisely this harshness is necessary" (ibid, pp. 263–64).

Nietzsche is quick to point out that the spread of religion comes at a high cost. He mentions in particular the price Europe has paid for Christianizing its people, but evidently the lesson also applies to the religion the superman will establish in the politics of the future. Over time religions founded to serve as tools of politics strongly incline to insubordination: they "insist on having their own *sovereign way*, . . . they themselves want to be ultimate ends and not means among other means" (*BGE* 62, p. 264). The political order that contains any religion thus has an *imperium in imperio*. Nietzsche makes no exception for Aristotle's recommendation to restrict the priesthood to old and wealthy men, probably because Aristotle only attenuates the problem without solving it. As a consequence of the revolutionary tendency of every religion including even the political religion established by the superman, religion's delicate function of enhancing and preserving the higher men above all is likely to be disrupted. When religion becomes independent of politics, it will likely favor the failures, the sick, and the degenerates. Thus Nietzsche tacitly acknowledges that built into his great politics are the seeds of its own destruction.

Nietzsche's great politics or "best regime" has three classes: the Brahmin-like philosophers of the future, under them the actual rulers, and, forming the base of the pyramid, the great multititude, the herd. That Plato likewise has three classes in his best regime is well known: the philosopher king(s), subordinate to them the auxiliaries or guardians, and on the bottom rung the great multitude of craftsmen and farmers, the wage earners. Considering the open disagreements between Plato and Nietzsche about the true and the good, the correspondence between their political "ideals" is remarkable. Plato's Socrates might well suggest that the parallel emerges from nature's asserting itself across the centuries. Is it not a kind of natural justice that requires this preposterous thing, that philosophers rule? Does not nature necessarily determine most crucial choices in the optimal political order? Nietzsche finds it impossible to answer these questions in the negative, but the affirmative raises difficulties for him because of his paradoxical stance toward nature. Appropriately, he goes on to treat nature and morality in chapter 5, "Toward a Natural History of Morals." Notwithstanding any concessions he might have to make to Plato, however, Nietzsche would insist that the first goal of his politics of the future is by no means the common good.

Chapter 4, "Sayings and Interludes," consists of 123 brief and apparently unconnnected aphorisms. Although one can discover ligatures here and there in this chapter, close inspection does not reveal an underlying order beneath the apparent chaos of the whole. All the aphorisms can be said to share a common theme, namely human psychology; but to identify this "common theme" is not to discover the sought unity within the apparent multiplicity, because according to the doctrine of the will to power, the study of *all things* reduces to human psychology. And the profound and daring thinker who plunges into the Nietzschean sea of the human psyche will find it bottomless and largely opaque. At any rate it seems to us that the links within chapter 4 are only occasional and not fundamental; that only by an implausible construction could one tightly connect the opening and closing aphorisms of the chapter; that the most likely indicators of "parts" of chapter 4, i.e., those aphorisms with italicized headings (*BGE* 83, p. 271; *BGE* 87, p. 272; *BGE* 140, p. 278; and *BGE* 165, p. 281), in no way provide thematic divisions of the chapter; and that even the numerically central aphorisms point to the unknowability of the whole.

Those numerically central aphorisms are 124, 125, and 126. On the face these three have nothing in common, apart from human psychology; for that matter, only by digging beneath the surface can we come to see that *BGE* 126 is primarily a psychological statement. On closer inspection all three central aphorisms prove to be about the decisiveness of becoming. In aphorism 125, which appears to be a lighthearted spoof but has its deeply serious side, Nietzsche observes that we resent having to unlearn and relearn. Here the object of the unlearning and relearning (*umlernen*) is "someone" (*jemand*), but in aphorism 126 the word "nature" occurs. Perhaps Nietzsche already has "nature" in mind in aphorism

125. Paragraph 126 reads, "A people is a detour of nature to get to six or seven great men. —Yes, and then to get around them." "Nature" is unambiguously synonomous with becoming or history. Nietzsche's surface intention here is to squelch the pretensions of every people (*Volk*) to be great in itself—a people, like a woman, is at best but a means for the generation of a very few great men. But Nietzsche indicates clearly that nature or history finally cannot be the standard by which peoples are judged, for the river of time not only flows in the direction of great men, but rolls just as irresistibly past them. Likewise, in the most important central aphorism of chapter 4, nature or becoming appears as something to be "overcome"; the subject of aphorism 124 is a noble death. "Whoever rejoices on the very stake triumphs not over pain but at the absence of pain he had expected. A parable." This parable is highly mysterious. Its seemingly incomprehensible character derives from our certainty that anyone who dies on the stake suffers excruciating pain. The parable is against nature. The literal message involves a willful denial of the necessity of excruciating pain. To state the paradox, then, is to begin to unriddle it: He who rejoices on the stake triumphs at the absence of pain because to deny pain with sufficient spiritedness is to abolish it. (Compare Zarathustra's advice to the shepherd in *Zarathustra* III, "On the Vision and the Riddle," 2.) To whom, then, is the man who rejoices on the stake likened? To the most noble man of all, to Zarathustra. Zarathustra's world of the eternal recurrence is related to the wisdom of Silenus "even as the rapturous vision of the tortured martyr to his suffering" (*The Birth of Tragedy* 3, p. 42, q.v.; this section may be the most useful passage to peruse when interpreting *BGE* 124.)

Elsewhere in the largely chaotic chapter 4 we restrict ourselves to a few favorite aphorisms that shed light on Nietzsche's project of educating toward the philosophers of the future. The first paragraph of the chapter, aphorism 63, asserts that the true teacher (the "teacher from the ground up") is a human being for whom devotion to his students is central to his whole life. At least with respect to his students, the genuine teacher is wholly altruistic. Nietzsche gives no examples of the genuine teacher, but when we cast about for one, our hook catches onto a description of Plato in *Twilight of the Idols*. In "Skirmishes of an Untimely Man" (23) Nietzsche contends that Plato "says" that he would not have philosophized at all had it not been for the presence of beautiful young men in Athens: "It is only their sight that transposes the philosopher's soul into an erotic trance, leaving it no peace until it lowers the seed of all exalted things into such beautiful soil." It is the "philosophic eroticism" of Nietzsche's Plato that leads to the development of dialectics. Since Nietzsche himself is a great lover, this characterization of Plato is not in itself a complaint. As we have already noticed, "[w]hatever is done out of love always occurs beyond good and evil" (*BGE* 153). Just as in the case of Nietzsche's Plato, Nietzsche's beloved and his students are indistinguishable, although the latter exist not in close proximity but in the unspecified future. They are the philosophers of the future. On the surface Nietzsche seems to love them as much as Plato loves the best of the Athenian youths, so what complaint can Nietzsche have against the genuine teacher that Plato represents? We suspect that whereas Nietzsche's erotic Plato loses himself in his love for his students, i.e., takes himself seriously only in relation to them, Nietzsche loves the philosophers of the future *strictly* as an affirmation of himself. Whereas Plato's love as portrayed is erotic, Nietzsche's is spirited. Nietzsche finds the erotic love that moves the genuine teacher not only disloyal to the self but ultimately even impossible. Nietzsche's Plato calls *himself* a teacher from the ground up and a pristinely erotic man, but Nietzsche does not entirely believe him. "One does not trust one's ears, even if one should trust Plato . . . Philosophy after the fashion of Plato might rather be defined as an erotic contest, as a further development and turning inward of the ancient agonistic gymnastics and of its presuppositions. What ultimately grew out of the philosophic eroticism of Plato? A new art form of the Greek *agon* . . ." (*Twilight*, "Skirmishes" 23). Nietzsche looks into Plato's soul and sees *thumos* domineering over *eros*. The purely erotic man is an empty ideal, for the essence of life is the will to power. It is probably no accident that the discussion of Plato's eroticism is followed by an attack on "*l'art pour l'art*" and that the paragraph on the genuine teacher is followed by an attack on "knowledge for its own sake."

One of the most sparkling and penetrating aphorisms is paragraph 102. "Discovering that one is loved in return really ought to disenchant the lover with the beloved. 'What? This person is modest enough to love even you? Or stupid enough? Or—or—'" (cf. *BGE* 86, p. 272). The beloved of Alpha is Beta. Alpha should be disenchanted with Beta upon discovering that Beta also loves Alpha. Alpha ought to be disenchanted because Alpha should know that there must be something wrong with Beta if Beta loves Alpha. In the first case Beta is unduly modest, i.e., Beta lacks self-knowledge. In the second case Beta fails to observe the gross defects of Alpha, and this lack of knowledge of Alpha establishes Beta's stupidity. In the third and most interesting case, which Nietzsche leaves to the reader's ingenuity, knowledge of neither Alpha nor Beta is lacking on the part of Beta. Beta is aware of Beta's own strengths, such as they are, and of the weaknesses of Alpha; but out of a desperate need to love, Beta loves Alpha in spite of Beta's knowledge. In the first case Beta loves out of un-called-for modesty, and in the second case out of stupidity, but in the third case out of sickness. This aphorism confirms Nietzsche's presumptuous claim to write in sentences what other men write in books. But does not the profundity of his insight here require, as the standard for judging love, the truly lovable, some notion of goodness that is in principle independent of the will to power?

Whatever the case might be, in chapter 4 Nietzsche generally paints life and love in very dark colors. At times his melancholy seems to surface undisguised, as when he extols the comforting effect of the thought of suicide (*BGE* 157, p. 281), or when he mentions the horrible corrosive power of the abyss (*BGE* 146, p. 279, *BGE* 89, p. 272). He indicates that self-deception is deplorable (*BGE* 68, p. 270, *BGE* 102, p. 274) but necessary (*BGE* 107, p. 274, *BGE* 138, p. 278). Self-knowledge is desirable (*BGE* 63 and 64, p. 269) but impossible (*BGE* 80 and 81, p. 271). Man's sexual impulse reaches up to the peaks of his soul (*BGE* 75, p. 271), but harmonious understanding between man and woman is impossible (*BGE* 85, p. 272, *BGE* 131, p. 277), and woman's heart is filled with spite and self-loathing (*BGE* 115, p. 275, *BGE* 139, p. 278, *BGE* 86, p. 272, and *BGE* 148, pp. 279–80; cf. *BGE* 84, p. 272). And, supposing truth is a woman, truth is deadly (*BGE* 152, p. 280, *BGE* 177, p. 283). In spite of all these spirited cries of doom and gloom, Nietzsche warns that we should not accuse him of malice toward humanity (*BGE* 184, p. 284); the development of the deepest pessimism will lead to the coming of the superman. The coming of the superman ought not to be, but doubtless will be, resisted out of the petty jealousy of an egalitarian spirit (*BGE* 185, p. 284).

Nietzsche says that "whatever has value in our world now does not have value in itself, according to its nature—nature is always valueless, but has been given value at some time, as a present—and it was we who gave and bestowed it." That observation would serve well as an epigraph to chapter 5 of *BGE*. In this chapter Nietzsche purports to present the natural history of morality, an altogether descriptive history of morality that eschews the predisposition in favor of a rational foundation for morality. This so-called natural, descriptive history of morality has hardly begun before Nietzsche points to Schopenhauer's flute playing as inconsistent with his supposed pessimism—a charge that assumes that flute playing as an indulgence in certain passions is life-affirming, and thus a charge that quietly presupposes a particular moral interpretation of the meaning of life (*BGE* 186, pp. 287–89). As the chapter develops, the moral notions that color Nietzsche's whole history of morals become more and more obtrusive. Socratic morality is attacked as crude and plebeian (*BGE* 190, p. 293). The Jews are blamed for (and credited with?) disparaging this world (*BGE* 195, p. 298). Cesare Borgia and other men of prey are deemed healthy, and Alcibiades, Caesar, and Frederick II are proclaimed beautiful (*BGE* 197, pp. 298–99, *BGE* 200, p. 302). Is this discussion truly the natural history of morality, or do we not rather encounter here a *uniquely Nietzschean* history? It appears that, consistent with the doctrine of the will to power, Nietzsche's will replaces nature in chapter 5. And yet Nietzsche speaks, and must speak, of "the moral imperative of nature," the imperative for a narrowing of perspective for the sake of life, the imperative for tyrannical dominion and slavish obedience (*BGE* 188). Nietzsche's morality relies on both nature and the denial of nature.

The same paradox in Nietzsche's thought occurs with respect to justice. Nietzsche deemphasizes justice in his treatment of morality, and justice is not one of his cardinal virtues, namely courage, insight, sympathy, and solitude (*BGE* 284). (The earlier list of four in the *Dawn* 556 also excludes justice: courage, probity, politeness, and generosity.) Sympathy, a passion, takes the place of justice in Plato's *Republic*. The principal explanation for Nietzsche's demotion of justice occurs in *The Genealogy of Morals*, where Nietzsche agrees with Hobbes that justice is merely conventional (II, 8–11).

'Just' and 'unjust' exist . . . only after the institution of the law . . .
To speak of just or unjust *in itself* is quite senseless; *in itself*, of
course, no injury, assault, exploitation, destruction can be 'unjust,'
since life operates *essentially*, that is in its basic functions, through
injury, assault, exploitation, destruction and simply cannot be
thought of at all without this character. One must, indeed, grant
something even more unpalatable: that, from the highest biological
standpoint, legal conditions can never be other than *exceptional conditions*, since they constitute a partial restriction of the will of life,
which is bent upon power, and are subordinate to its total goal as a
single means: namely, as a means of creating *greater* units of power.

In spite of this rejection of natural justice, Nietzsche does have a
complaint against Hobbes, namely that he is ignoble, that Hobbes
fails to do justice to nobility. In chapter 9 of *BGE* Nietzsche remarks
that the name the noble soul gives to its egoism is "justice itself"
(*BGE* 265). This justice is conceived as a part of "the primordial law
of things," and the equal privileges the noble soul shares with its
equals, including the exchange of honors and rights with them, is
"of the nature of all social relations and thus also belongs to the natural condition of things" (*BGE* 265, p. 405). The principle of natural justice is giving equally to equals and unequally to unequals. To
this formal principle of justice Nietzsche gives substantive meaning
through an analysis of his historical context. Broadly speaking, that
context is the decline of the West into nihilism, a decline that car-
ries with it the opportunity for cultivating the highest human possibilities. A major political symptom of the decline of the West is the
democratic-socialistic movement of Nietzsche's time. In such an era
it becomes urgent to emphasize "natural" inequality of excellences
among men and "natural" inequity of rewards due them. The need
likewise arises to denounce the Christian morality behind democracy and socialism—the morality of fearfulness and hatred, including self-hatred (cf. *BGE* 49, p. 254)—and to attack herd morality as
the predecessor of the slave morality of the Christians. "Natural justice" requires suppression of the rabble and exaltation of the higher
men.

The formula "give equally to equals and unequally to unequals"
is Aristotelian, of course, and Aristotle presents it as a timeless principle of justice: constant nature rather than fickle history provides
the standard for judging human beings and their actions. For Nietz-

sche the measure of equality and inequality is not natural human excellence as expressed in the virtues discussed in the *Nicomachean Ethics*, and certainly not the natural supremacy of human reason over the passions—in his depiction Socrates himself knows in his heart of hearts that reason must inevitably serve the passions (*BGE* 191, pp. 293–94). The standard for Nietzsche is the full development of the most tyrannical passions, nay, of the single most tyrannical passion, the will to power. This standard is natural in that nature simply is the will to power (*BGE* 188, pp. 290–92, *BGE* 192, pp. 294–95, *The Will to Power* 1067). But do not democracies express the will to power just as much as do aristocracies and tyrannies? According to Nietzsche and Machiavelli alike, all regimes are ultimately tyrannies. Nevertheless, it is the tyrant in the most obvious sense, Cesare Borgia, whom Nietzsche calls the "natural" man (*BGE* 197, pp. 298–99). (According to Plato's Socrates in Republic IX, the shameless tyrant is in crucial respects an unnatural man.) A natural hierarchy evidently determines Nietzsche's preference, and not the other way around. Nietzsche makes this point more explicit in *Antichrist* 57:

> The *order of castes*, the supreme, the dominant law, is merely the sanction of a *natural order*, a natural lawfulness of the first rank, over which no arbitrariness, no "modern idea," has any power. In every healthy society there are three types that condition each other and gravitate differently physiologically; each has its own hygiene, its own field of work, its own sense of perfection and mastery. Nature . . . distinguishes the preeminently spiritual ones, those who are preeminently strong in muscle and temperament, and those, the third type, who excel neither in one respect nor in the other, the mediocre ones—the last as the great majority, the first as the elite. The highest caste—I call them the *fewest*—being perfect, also has the privileges of the fewest: Among them, to represent happiness, beauty, and graciousness on earth. Only to the most spiritual human beings is beauty permitted: among them alone is graciousness not weakness. *Pulchrum est paucorum hominum*: the good is a privilege. On the other hand, there is nothing that they may be conceded less than ugly manners or a pessimistic glance, an eye that makes ugly—or indignation at the total aspect of things. Indignation is the privilege of the chandalas; pessimism, too. *"The world is perfect"*—thus says the instinct of the most spiritual, the Yes-saying instinct: "imperfection, whatever is beneath us, distance, the pathos of distance—even the

chandala still belongs to this perfection." The most spiritual men, as
the *strongest*, find their happiness where others would find their destruction: in the labyrinth, in hardness against themselves and others,
in experiments; their joy is self-conquest; asceticism becomes in
them nature, need, and instinct. Difficult tasks are a privilege to
them; to play with burdens that crush others, a recreation. Knowledge—a form of asceticism. They are the most venerable kind of
man; that fact does not preclude their being the most cheerful and the
kindliest. They rule not because they want to but because they *are*;
they are not free to be second. The *second*: They are the guardians
of the law, those who see to order and security, the noble warriors,
and above all the king as the highest formula of warrior, judge, and
upholder of the law. The second or the executive arm of the most
spiritual, what is closest to them and belongs to them, what does
everything gross in the work of ruling for them—their retinue, their
right hand, their best pupils. In all this, to repeat, there is nothing arbitrary, nothing contrived; whatever is *different* is contrived—
contrived for the ruin of nature. The order of castes, the *order of
rank*, merely formulates the highest law of life; the separation of the
three types as necessary for the preservation of society, to make possible the higher and the highest types. The *inequality* of rights is the
first condition for the existence of any rights at all. A right is a privilege. A man's state of being is his privilege. Let us not underestimate the privileges of the *mediocre*. As one climbs *higher*, life becomes even harder; the coldness increases, responsibility increases.
A high culture is a pyramid: It can stand only on a broad base; its
first presupposition is a strong and soundly consolidated mediocrity.
Handicraft, trade, agriculture, *science*, the greatest part of art, the
whole quintessence of *professional* activity, to sum it up, is compatible only with the mediocre amount of ability and ambition; that sort
of thing would be out of place among exceptions; the instinct here
required would contradict both aristocratism and anarchism. To be a
public utility, a will, a function, for that one must be destined by nature: It is *not* society, it is the only kind of *happiness* of which the
great majority are capable that makes intelligent machines out of
them. For the mediocre, to be mediocre is their happiness; mastery
of one thing, specialization—a natural instinct.

Following his own doctrine, Nietzsche would of course deny that
the natural order he has discovered, however strikingly it might
resemble Plato's natural order, is available to the best human beings in all ages. Man must first reach a certain stage of historical

development. The centuries old law of Manu, described in the above passage, does not properly understand the natural order, because Manu does not know that the superman stands at the apex. Manu arises before the development of the historical sense and the turning in upon itself of the will to power. Knowledge of the deepest truth about the natural order was impossible prior to the genesis of the first genuine quest for self-knowledge, which entails self-overcoming. But can any such "natural order" be anything other than mere human creation if it changes through history according to the fluctuating dictates of the will? Is the so-called natural order merely Nietzsche's preference after all, or can he defend its deeper naturalness?

The sixth, seventh, and eighth chapters of *BGE* are devoted to Nietzsche's project of educating toward the superman. Unlike Plato's Socrates and like Karl Marx, Nietzsche apparently wishes and even strives to bring about his ideal concretely. If he were not such an activist, we might think of *Romans* 8:25: "If we hope for that we see not, then do we with patience wait for it." At any rate, in "We Scholars" Nietzsche expressly speaks of his concern about "the dangers for a philosopher's development." Scholarship must be excoriated expressly for the sake of bringing about new philosophers from among the scholars; every new philosopher must first be a scholar. All scholars must recognize once again the masterfulness of philosophy, and the best of them must transcend ignoble specialization and avoid the pitfalls of shallow dilettantism and unmanly skepticism in order for philosophers of the future to come about. Nietzsche desires to instill in his new philosopher-nobles the will to dominion: genuine philosophers are commanders and legislators, and their so-called will to truth is actually will to power (*BGE* 204–11, pp. 311–26). Zarathustra exclaims, "O my brothers, like a fresh roaring wind Zarathustra comes . . And you shall learn solely in order to create. And you shall first learn from me how to learn— how to learn well. He that has ears to hear, let him hear" (*Zarathustra* III, "On Old and New Tablets," *BGE* 16, p. 318).

Zarathustra is a Caesarian breeder and cultural man of violence, who should not be confused with the scholar. His superman, Nietzsche's philosopher of the future, is the man in whom the rest of existence is justified (*BGE* 207, p. 318; cf. *BGE* 258, p. 392 and *The Will to Power* 997).

The scholar is a different man. He is a dependent being, not self-sufficient. Since he is an instrument, his activity can be justified only by the end he serves; indeed his activity is impossible apart from this end. For the scholar cannot function unless he can distinguish the meaningful from the meaningless, and he does this on the basis of what is valuable, truth: The truth guides him. The value of truth, however, is not created by him, and this is precisely its value—it is beyond the world of change.

If one were to take "truth" from him, the scientist would thus become an impossibility. But Nietzsche does exactly this, by questioning truth, by understanding it as problematical. The scholar must therefore receive a new meaning in justification, and that is given him by . . . the philosopher of the future: Scholarship from now on can have meaning from *within* Nietzsche's philosophy, but not outside it. The new scholar determines the former creations of value and presses them into formulas, an overcoming of the past which is a labor preliminary to the philosopher's creation of values. But performing it depends on a decisive shift: The intellect's future "objectivity" can no longer be understood as "disinterested" contemplation, but, rather, as the ability to direct one's affirmations and denials so that one can use a variety of perspectives and interpretations in the attempt to know.[13]

Chapter 6 begins with complaints against scholars and ends with a discussion of what it means to be a philosopher, and constitutes an effort to refine the virtues of scholarship and to raise scholars to their highest possibilities, even beyond scholarship. Chapter 7, "Our Virtues," continues this effort at education by refining the virtues of the free spirits. Nietzsche's contemporaries are men of the historical sense, "unpretentious, selfless, modest, courageous, full of self-overcoming, full of devotion, very grateful, very patient, very accommodating," and thus men out of touch with nobility (*BGE* 224, p. 342). Of these putative virtues Nietzsche tries to abrogate all but courage (and by implication self-overcoming). Courage appears to be *the* noble virtue. It next turns out, however, that probity is "our virtue" par excellence. Courage and probity, we will learn, are not distinguishable virtues for Nietzsche: "In all desire to know there is a drop of cruelty" (*BGE* 229, p. 349). If one cannot seek knowledge without being cruel to oneself, without hurting the basic will of one's spirit, why seek knowledge at all? Why consider probity a virtue (*BGE* 30, p. 352 and generally pp. 349–52)? Nietzsche directly confronts us with this question in chapter 7 and then quickly drops it, perhaps because he wishes to delay fuller treatment of the problem of the self until he takes up nobility thematically.

Hereafter Nietzsche's educational project becomes more obscure, probably in anticipation of chapter 9 on nobility. "Our Virtues" ends with an assortment of considerations on women that apparently has no direct connection to the virtues of the free-spirited, except that this discussion does remind us both that a human being can have virtues only in accordance with his or her nature and that nature is problematical. It may be that the two parts of the chapter are complementary. The first part of chapter 7 teaches that the virtue of man is courage or manliness; the second, that the virtue of woman is the bringing forth of great men, or womanliness. The decay of European culture that surrounds Nietzsche can be described as the womanization of men and the denaturing of women. In chapter 7 Nietzsche strives to arrest, even reverse, that decay.

Nietzsche has emphasized in the chapter on the free spirit that free-spiritedness is incompatible with fatherlandishness. It is important for a free spirit "not to remain stuck to a fatherland" (*BGE* 41, p. 242). Chapter 8, "Peoples and Fatherlands," continues the refinement of the virtues of the prospective nobility by purging fatherlandishness from the souls of future philosophers. This quite political, though not merely political, chapter does give negative advice, but can one also extract a positive teaching? To answer this question we must investigate the meaning of the good European and look ahead to the chapter on nobility.

"Peoples and Fatherlands" is the most obviously political chapter in *BGE*.[14] In chapter 8 Nietzsche calls for a united Europe, but union alone will not suffice. Rejecting the possibilities offered by Bismarck and by socialism, he insists upon a union of good Europeanism (*BGE* 241, pp. 364–65, *BGE* 242, pp. 366–67). Since such a union can come about only through heavy reliance on the Germans, the Jews, the French, and the English, Nietzsche treats each of those peoples in turn in chapter 8. But what is the meaning of good Europeans? They are members of a united Europe devoted to a new and higher *reason* (*BGE* 242, p. 366, *together with BGE* 201, pp. 303–4), members led, it is true, by powerful dictators and warlords, but adherents to the "old faith that only a great thought can give a deed or cause greatness" (*BGE* 241, p. 365). Bismarck is not great, because he is inexperienced in and unequipped for philosophy. But truly great men, truly great *tyrants*, are on the horizon. Precisely the democratization of Europe, the process of the "evolving European," fosters the development of "exceptional human beings of the most dangerous and attractive quality" (*BGE* 242, p. 366), and the mediocre multitudes of modern, sick-willed Europeans will long for strong men to enslave them. "The democratization of Europe is at the same time an involuntary arrangement for the cultivation of tyrants—taking that word in every sense, including the most spiritual" (*BGE* 242, p. 367). The road to the last man can also be the road to the superman. To this prospect of good Europeanism Nietzsche gives not only applause but also cosmic support: "I hear with pleasure that our sun is swiftly moving toward the constellation of Hercules—and I hope that man on this earth will in this respect follow the sun's example? And we first of all, we good Europeans!" (*BGE* 243, p. 367).

Contemporary Germany is the most powerful nation in Nietzsche's time, and accordingly—not just because of his own nationality—deserves the most criticism. "The word 'German' is constantly being used nowadays, to advocate nationalism and race-hatred and to be able to take pleasure in the national scabies of the heart and the blood-poisoning that now leads the nations of Europe to delimit and barricade themselves against each other as if it were a matter of quarantine." (*The Gay Science* V, 377). Germany of today means ponderousness and boorishness and psychic disorder (*BGE* 244, pp. 367–70). These defects could be remedied in part by the "centuries old great European taste of Mozart" with his "tender enthusiasms . . . his courtesy of the heart, his longing for the graceful, those in love, those dancing, those easily moved to tears, his faith in the South (*BGE* 245, p. 370; "the South" of course refers to southern Europe). But Mozart has been replaced by the fatherlandish Schumann; as the swansong of "the good old time," Mozart offers no hope for the revival of Europe. Nevertheless, Nietzsche's admiration for Mozart and for the South does reveal that Nietzsche's educational project, like that of Socrates in Plato's *Republic*, involves a softening as well as a hardening of men. Nietzsche's de-emphasis of the need for softening men is not derived solely from his historical situation, from the peculiar womanization of European man. For courage or hardness is the ostensible core of nobility, and neither moderation nor justice is a virtue (*BGE* 284, p. 416, *BGE* 260, pp. 394–98). "The noble human being honors himself as one who is powerful, also as one who has power over himself, who knows how to speak and be silent, who delights in being severe and hard with himself and respects all severity and hardness. 'A hard heart Wotan put into my breast,' says an old Scandinavian saga: a fitting poetic expression, seeing that it comes from the soul of a proud Viking" (*BGE* 260, p. 395).

The elevation of man out of German narrowness into good Europeanism requires a revival of literature and of oratory as well as of their audiences. The Germans can no longer write, read, speak, or listen. Great writing has a delicacy, richness, and daring of tempo that is incomprehensible to Germans contemporary to Nietzsche. The greatest writing is in fact meant to be read aloud, "with a resounding voice: that means, with all the crescendoes, inflections, and reversals of tone and changes in tempo in which the ancient public world took delight" (*BGE* 247, p. 373). Apparently great literature and great oratory are both exercises in manliness, like the movements of the swordsman who experiences "the dangerous delight of the quivering, ever-sharp blade that desires to bite, hiss, cut" (*BGE* 246, p. 373), and unlike Platonic *musikē*.

The Germans merit so much attention not only because of their current ascendancy in Europe but also because they are a begetter people, a manly people. Nietzsche names two other begetter peoples, the Jews and the Romans—and he asks whether, rather than asserts that, the Germans are such causers of new orders of life (*BGE* 248, p. 374). The Jews gave mankind Christ, and the Romans gave us Caesar. Nietzsche intimates here "in all modesty" that the new order contributed by the Germans is the order of the superman, Caesar with the soul of Christ, i.e., that the Germans can become a begetter people *only* through the activity of Nietzsche. His hope is that through him Germany will father the revival of Europe, with France especially as mother. But Nietzsche is no naive visionary. He has no illusions about the difficulties of joining begetter peoples to birth-giving peoples, about the Tartuffery of every people, or even about the possibility of self-knowledge toward which the good European aspires (*BGE* 248 and 249, p. 375). Good Europeanism will be so far from the anti-Jewish madness rampant in Germany as to involve an alliance with the Jews. Nietzsche respects the Jews for their revaluation of values, for their grand style in morality, and for their strength and resilience (*BGE* 250, p. 375, *BGE* 251, pp. 377–78). In contrast, the English are so shallow and mediocre that they are fit for little or nothing better than slavery to the new caste of nobles whom Nietzsche hopes to bring into rule over Europe (*BGE* 252, pp. 379–80, *BGE* 253, pp. 381–82). Nietzsche gives special emphasis to the plebianism of modern ideas, which he blames on the English. He appears to have in mind especially democratic utilitarianism, the English synthesis of Socratism with herd morality. Utilitarianism, a morality of fear, subordinates the good of those who are independent and superior to the good of the greatest number or the herd, to the common good. Thus the utilitarianism of the English is quintessential ignobility. France, however, will rank high within the new nobility, for the most spiritual culture and most elevated tastes in Europe are French: The French have artistic passions, a moralistic culture, and a temperament that synthesizes North and South (*BGE* 254, pp. 382–85). Thus from the French the good European will take love of beauty, discipline, psychological sensitivity, and transnationalism.

The transnationalism of the French, and in particular their discovery of "a piece of the South in music," suggests to Nietzsche the possibility or dream of a new Mozart and a new transnational music beyond good and evil—the music of the superman. Albeit unconsciously, Europe's aspiration to become one far surpasses the shallow Christianity of Richard Wagner's music (*BGE* 256, pp. 386–88). This new music that Nietzsche imagines would, presumably as a by-product of the historical sense (*BGE* 186, pp. 287–89, *BGE* 223, p. 340, *BGE* 224, pp. 341–42), transcend morality and yet be hospitable to fugitives from the setting moral world (*BGE* 254, pp. 384–85, *BGE* 255, p. 385; cf. *BGE* 250, p. 375). The music of the overman and his servants, i.e., the music of the good Europeans, is the music of magnanimity. Good Europeanism is the synthesis of the highest passion with the highest reason.[15] It is quite clear that Nietzsche connects his aspirations for higher men to Europe because Europe is the home of Western civilization.

Nietzsche's teaching on nobility must bear a heavy burden: among other things, it must lay bear the heart of Nietzschean politics if his promise to instigate great politics can be taken seriously. The first aphorisms of chapter 9 do indeed have a political appearance. Nietzsche's nobles are rulers in the obvious sense. They are proud, self-regarding, and tyrannical, and although they are well-mannered among themselves, they contemn their inferiors. As for superiors, they recognize none — least of all gods. Tough and intolerant, also warlike, the nobles exploit their underlings as slaves to the will of the nobility. It seems no exaggeration to call them ruthless, and it would serve us to compare them to Aristotle's more proper magnanimous man. Are these Nietzschean aristocrats also philosophers? Nietzsche does follow his discussion of the aristocracy with a new consideration of philosophy, but there he apparently is no longer talking about the aforementioned aristocrats. As it develops, the discussion of nobility becomes increasingly remote from politics: philosophers at any given time will be too few in number to constitute a ruling class, and the inner meaning of philosophy seems to be far, far removed from community affairs. That inner meaning cannot be separated from the philosopher's suffering, or at the very least *Nietzsche's* philosophy seems inseparable from *his* suffering. And ultimately that inner meaning remains inaccessible to anyone but the philosopher — worse, at least partially inaccessible even to the philosopher himself. The book ends shrouded in mystery.

Why does Nietzsche suffer, and what connects the apolitical part to the political part of the chapter on nobility? That question would seem critical for the interpretation of *Beyond Good and Evil*. Partly, as we have already indicated, Nietzsche suffers because of the inaccessibility of the self. In other words, his pain derives in part from the unavailability of truth. But no less he suffers over the mortality of the self. As we have indicated in our interpretation of the eternal recurrence, under his mask Nietzsche recoils in horror at the truth that he, that the whole human race, will die (cf. Plato *Symposium* 207A, 208B-C). Not so much that truth is beyond reach but that truth is ugly overwhelms him. Horror at death contributes to the hopeless desire to will the eternal recurrence, and horror at death moves him to educate his children, philosophers of the future, for noble rule — albeit indirectly, through a lesser but more conspicuous aristocracy — over politics. To be sure, this Nietzsche, too, may ultimately prove to be a persona, an irony, a mask.[16] And what of Zarathustra? Zarathustra's name never appears in the text proper of *Beyond Good and Evil*, and occurs only once in the Aftersong at the end; this oddity may signify some discrepancy between Zarathustra's nobility and Nietzsche's noble soul. In *Thus Spoke Zarathustra*, Zarathustra whispers to Life that he will return to Life, suggesting that for at least a moment Zarathustra believes, as Nietzsche's noble soul can never believe, in the eternal recurrence. So viewed, Zarathustra is Nietzsche's unattainable ideal in whom the suffering of Nietzsche's noble soul is transcended by joy. Zarathustra is thus the comic solution to the Nietzschean tragedy of life.[17]

But what could lie still deeper in Nietzsche's soul than the masks of comedy and tragedy? "One should not be misled: all great thinkers are skeptics. Zarathustra is a skeptic" (*Antichrist* 54). The unmasking continues: "Strength, *freedom* which is born of the strength and overstrength of the spirit, proves itself by skepticism. Men of conviction"—including the superman—"are not worthy of the last consideration in fundamental questions of value and disvalue. Convictions are prisons. . . . A spirit who wants great things is necessarily a skeptic" (ibid.). We now can begin to fathom why the final strokes of Nietzsche's brush have motley caresses and fifty yellows and browns and greens: Regrettably, his written and painted thoughts are about to become immortalized as truths, his free-spirited philosophizing will soon become a collection of "Nietzschean verities," a philosophy (*BGE* 256, pp. 426–27). The incomparable richness, the indescribable beauty, the fiery vitality of his mortal activity, the philosophic life, preoccupy him now—as ever. If he can joyfully affirm all of nature (Xenophon, *Symposium* ii. 19), he says "yes" less to its unknowable eternity than to what he knows very well: that nature makes the human peaks, and thus necessarily the human valleys, possible and good. In this affirmation and none other consists the sublimest conquest of the spirit of revenge, the truest Nietzschean nobility of all. "And we should consider every day lost on which we have not danced at least once. And we should consider every truth false that was not accompanied by at least one laugh" (*Zarathustra* III, "On Old and New Tablets," 23). *Nietzsche*: Zarathustra in front, and superman behind, but in the middle—Socrates.

Notes

1. Quoted in Karl Reinhardt, "Nietzsche's Lament of Ariadne," trans. Gunther Heilbrunn, in *Interpretation: A Journal of Political Philosophy*,

VI, No. 3 (October, 1977), 216. Cf. *Ecce Homo*, "Why I Am a Destiny,"1: "There is nothing in me of a founder of a religion."

The thesis of this chapter about the eternal recurrence was first advanced by the author of the present book in a doctoral dissertation at the University of Chicago in 1979. Independently, Professor Stanley Rosen has reached a similar conclusion in his provocative *The Mask of Enlightenment: Nietzsche's Zarathustra* (Cambridge, Mass.: Cambridge University Press, 1995). (On Nietzsche's relationship to the Enlightenment compare Heinz Röttges, *Nietzsche und die Dialektik der Aufklärung* (Berlin: Walter de Gruyter, 1970), especially pp. 222–92. Rosen correctly portrays the will to power and the eternal return as myths and rightly describes Nietzsche's disciples as caricatures of supermen. However, Rosen's surreal Nietzsche paints life as an illusory dream (cf. *Dawn* 119), whereas the mature Nietzsche describes his task as wakefulness itself (*BGE* preface).

In contrast to Rosen, Lawrence Lampert in his *Nietzsche's Teaching: An Interpretation of Thus Spoke Zarathustra* (New Haven, Conn.: Yale University Press, 1986) and *Leo Strauss and Nietzsche*, (Chicago: University of Chicago Press, 1996) presents a surprisingly orthodox Nietzsche, a disciple of Zarathustra who in his heart of hearts fervently subscribes to the eternal recurrence and thereby gains his redemption. In *Thus Spoke Zarathustra*, however, Zarathustra urges his pupils *not* to remain disciples.

Regarding the eternal recurrence even Karl Löwith, whose pathbreaking work has opened horizons only tentatively explored in the present book, apparently undervalued Nietzsche's blanket assertion in *Antichrist* 54 that all great spirits are skeptics. The same applies to Karl-Heinz Volkmann-Schluck, author of *Die Philosophie Nietzsches: Der Untergang der abendlandischen Metaphysik* (Wurzburg, Germany: Konighausen and Neumann, 1991). Volkmann-Schluck brilliantly articulates connections between modern subjectivism and Nietzsche's organic life as will to power, but attaches too little weight to Nietzsche's characterization, e.g., in *BGE*, of that doctrine as *hypothetical*.

Peter Berkowitz in his *Nietzsche: The Ethics of an Immoralist* (Cambridge, Mass.: Harvard University Press, 1995), especially pp. 263–65, comes closest to our understanding of Nietzsche's intention. Berkowitz offers an intelligent but one-sided anthropological characterization of the eternal recurrence, and seems unduly to ignore its cosmological and ontological aspects. Thus, in his critique of Nietzsche's Zarathustra, Berkowitz sometimes risks appearing to be a *partisan* of reason. (On the other hand, considering our contemporary moral-political situation, Berkowitz might reply that today such risks are eminently worth taking.) See the balanced and judicious criticisms offered by Werner Dannhauser in his respectful book review in *First Things* 60 (February 1996), pp. 65–68.

2. See *BGE* 47, pp. 251–52 and Kaufmann's footnote 1 on page 247 of *Basic Writings*. See also note 13 to chapter 2 above. Ludwig Feuerbach wrote a book entitled *Das Wesen der Religion*. Nietzsche takes care to distinguish his understanding of religion from Feuerbach's.

3. We refer here to the original conclusion of *Zarathustra* at the end of part III. Part IV subtly distances Zarathustra from the recurrence and, less subtly, from the "higher men." See Gadamer, "The Drama of Zarathustra," pp. 227–31.

4. See our discussion of the second mask at pp. 95–97.

5. Recall note 2 above.

6. Leo Strauss, "Note on the Plan," p. 101.

7. Support for this contention will be indicated in the discussion of the eternal return.

8. Nietzsche also compares himself to Pascal in the preface, p. 193. Cf. *Ecce Homo*, "Why I Am So Clever," *BGE* 3, in *Basic Writings*, p. 699; *Selected Letters*, p. 327.

9. Does Nietzsche's stipulation of *human* soul imply that nonhuman beings also can have souls? If beings higher than men "possess" souls, would the history of divine soul be at least as interesting as the history of human soul to "a born psychologist?"

Central to his history of the human soul may be the question, seemingly briefly treated, "Why atheism today?" (*BGE* 53, p. 249). In *BGE* 54 he mentions that modern philosophy, though anti-Christian, is "to say this for the benefit of more refined ears, by no means anti-religious," p. 257. Nietzsche does not tell us here whether he looks with favor or disgruntlement on the religious instinct that he detects in modern philosophy, an instinct that has obviously survived despite the strong rational objections just stated in *BGE* 53. But earlier he has spoken of *das religiöse Wesen*, the "religious essence" or "the religious matter," as "the religious neurosis." He elaborates this indelicate hint in *Antichrist* 54:

> [T]he need for faith, for some kind of unconditional Yes and No . . . is a need born of *weakness*. The man of faith, the "believer" of every kind, is necessarily a dependent man—one who cannot posit *himself* as an end, one who cannot posit any end at all by himself. The "believer" does not belong to *himself*, he can only be a means, he must be *used up*, he requires somebody to use him up. His instinct gives the highest honor to a morality of self-abnegation; everything persuades him in this direction: his prudence, his experience, his vanity. Every kind of faith is itself an expression of self-abnegation, of self-alienation. If one considers how necessary most people find something regulatory, which will bind them from without and tie them down; how compulsion, *slavery* in a higher

sense, is the sole and ultimate condition under which the more weak-willed human being, woman in particular, can prosper—then one will also understand conviction, "faith." The man of conviction has his backbone in it. *Not* to see many things, to be impartial at no point, to be party through and through, to have a strict and necessary perspective in all questions of value—this alone makes it possible for this kind of human being to exist at all. But with this they are the opposite, the antagonists, of what is truthful—of truth. The believer is not free to have any conscience at all for questions of "true" and "untrue": to have integrity on *this* point would at once destroy him.

Portable Nietzsche, pp. 638–39. cf. BGE 208–10, pp. 318–25. (See also the last paragraph of this chapter and the appendix, below.) Modern philosophy, with its religious bent, is antiphilosophic. If the most powerful rational arguments against religion cannot purge modern "philosophy" of the religious neurosis, what can? Perhaps Nietzsche the psychologist and poet intends to manipulate and exaggerate the religious instinct so as to enable some to overcome it entirely, and thus to make authentic philosophy possible again?

Is Nietzsche's expression "*the* human soul" ultimately compatible with his previous definition of soul as "subjective multiplicity?" Presumably Nietzsche means "the human soul *as it were*," indicating nothing more than the range of human experiences (*BGE* 45, p. 249). Still, if a collection of experiences can appropriately be put under a single heading like "human soul," must they not have something critically important, perhaps even essential, in common?

10. Bernd Magnus, *Nietzsche's Existential Imperative* (Bloomington: Indiana University Press, 1978) elaborates on the internal contradiction between freedom and necessity involved in this responsibility.

11. See, e.g., Heidegger, *The End of Philosophy*, trans. Joan Stambaugh (New York: Harper and Row, Inc., 1973), especially the fourth chapter, pp. 84–110.

12. Joseph Cropsey, *Plato's World*, pp. 69–110. Cf. *Twilight*, "Reason in Philosophy" 2: "Heraclitus will remain eternally right with his assertion that Being is an empty fiction"; 4: "Everywhere 'Being' is projected by thought, pushed underneath as the cause; the concept of Being follows, and is a derivative of, the concept of ego"; 5: "nothing has possessed a more naive power of persuasion than the error concerning Being."

13. Mark Blitz, "Nietzsche and Political Science: The Problem of Politics," *Symposium: A Quarterly Journal in Modern Foreign Literatures*, 28, No. 1 (Spring, 1974), 74–75.

14. In paragraph 211 Nietzsche uses "moral" and "political" synonymously, thereby indicating the deeply political character of *BGE* altogether.

15. See Martin Heidegger, *What Is Called Thinking*, trans. J. Glenn Gray and F. Wieck (New York: Harper and Row, Harper Torch Books, 1968), pp. 58–60, 68–69; Leo Strauss, "Note on the Plan," p. 107.

16. See *BGE* 289: "The hermit does not believe that any philosopher . . . ever expressed his real and ultimate opinions in books." Cf. Plato's Seventh Letter 344A-D. To be Nietzsche's real children, the truest philosophers of the future would have to be not exemplars of the superman spoken of, but unbelieving free spirits of the future, whose genuine free-spiritedness has been fostered by Nietzsche's attacks on philosophy and religion.

17. See Löwith, *Nietzsche's Philosophy of The Eternal Recurrence*, pp. 180–81.

Appendix

Nietzsche and the Eternal Recurrence

"Docemur disputare, non vivere."
("We are taught how to discuss and debate, but not how to live.")

—*Seneca Epistulae morales* 95, 13

In the twentieth century "the plebeianism of the modern spirit, which is of English origin, erupted once again on its native soil . . ." (Nietzsche, *Genealogy of Morals*, I, 4). We stubborn Anglophones long resisted the philosophical movements of phenomenology and existentialism, Nietzsche's heirs, during the generations of their intellectual conquest of Europe. Our religious roots, our powerful moral attachments to democracy and to natural rights, may partly explain our evident reluctance to descend into such theoretical and psychological depths, beyond good and evil. Yet, the same laudable moral-political fortitude and love of liberty that have twice spared humanity the horrors of world tyranny have also unwittingly fostered the proliferation of various forms of relatively empty, trivial human life across the globe. No one aspires to greatness. If suddenly someone did, we would either sedate this strange person or race around like geese in our haste to persuade the renegade of the extreme folly of all great sacrifices, without which greatness cannot arise. Depriving life of greatness, however, has consequences: pusillanimity, boredom, indifference, lassitude, drugs, shrugs, and the ubiquitous expletive "Whatever." Our petty pleasures do persist, as do assorted frustrations and complaints; but what remains to uplift and inspire us? What in our time can still seize and transfigure us? What can we cherish with all our might and all our soul? What can give profound meaning to our lives? Nietzsche answers these questions, as it were, with a single word; a word that he wields as a lethal weapon against pre-Nietzschean modernity and as a plowshare for sowing the seeds of a new philosophy for the future: eternity.

God has already died at our hands, according to Nietzsche, so the new love of eternity will not satisfy a nostalgia for the good old days of revealed religion. Among other things, the tower of Babel, comprised of religious sects and a multitude of incompatible revelations, indicates to Nietzsche that we are bereft of a divinity who can communicate clearly. To be sure, God's death was a dreadful, earthshaking event. Nevertheless, the superman of the future who loves nothing more than eternity—understood as the never ending, identical repetition of all physical events of the universe in all details, including the most odious—this Nietzschean superman rebelliously exults in undisguised atheism.

As is familiar to everyone, Christianity and other Scriptural faiths paint a fundamentally progressive portrait of the course of the universe. Even if, seen through the lens of the New Testament, this world resembles a valley of tears, in the end the omnipotent will of God shall prevail, redeeming suffering and avenging evil. Nietzsche regards this understanding as nihilistic and pathological. He charges Christianity with nihilism because it radically depreciates the only life we certainly do have, life in this world, for the sake of an unknown afterlife. He adds the charge of psycho-pathology because of biblical Christianity's lust for bloody sacrifice and revenge. Christianity needs an eternal hell for sinners and even the crucifixion of the son of God. "Wrath is cruel, and anger is outrageous" (Proverbs 27:4). By contrast, the noble being without resentment, who wills the eternal recurrence of the same—a cyclical concept inherited from the ancient Pythagoreans, Empedocles, and Heraclitus—resoundingly affirms all that ever was, is, and will be. The liberation from the spirit of revenge, the reconciliation of man and the world, could hardly be more perfect.[1]

—Or could it? Martin Heidegger,[2] among others, accuses Nietzsche of succumbing to his own brand of nihilism and spirit of revenge. Despite his this-worldliness, with his teaching of eternal recurrence, Nietzsche no less than the Christians preaches an immortality—we shall all return, just as we are, again and again, forever—that lacks any empirical warrant. Also, as do the Christians, Nietzsche's superman avows his love for an eternity that, albeit nontranscendent in his case, exceeds human grasp and knowledge. The superman radically differs from the ancients in that he *wills* the eternal repetition of the selfsame. Yet one need not will a fact of nature. The conscious willing of a fiction, on the other hand, will always suffer from self-awareness and require self-deception. Nietzsche's effort to transcend Christian disaffection with the world and to establish a ground for psychic health seems to culminate in a bizarre form of atheistic religion involving extreme alienation and one of the most noxious diseases of the soul (Plato *Republic* 382a-b).

Heidegger's critique of Nietzsche as the nihilistic peak of the modern project to conquer nature could seem to suggest that the latter thinker argued for the validity of the eternal recurrence in metaphysical treatises. Actually, the principal development of the teaching occurs in *Thus Spoke Zarathustra*, a poetic work beyond compare. Hans-Georg Gadamer,[3] more sensitive to ironic playfulness than Heidegger, offers a most useful corrective by emphasizing the *drama* of Zarathustra. The titular character, named after the founder of the old Persian religion, does at first seem to speak on behalf of the sacred teaching of a new, godless theology of eternal recurrence. The only version of the book published in Nietzsche's lifetime concludes with "Seven Seals" (a hostile, mocking echo of the closing book of the Bible), in which Zarathustra seven times trumpets his love for eternity in a symbolic new creation of man and the whole. Nietzsche designated the originally unpublished "Fourth and Final Part" as "for my friends and not for the public." In Part IV, Zarathustra attests to his love for his animals, natural beings. But he complains that the so-called higher men, a comical, foul-smelling lot who worship the braying, yes-saying ass that represents the eternal return, slumber while he is awake. "These are not my proper companions," he exclaims. At the very end of the book, Zarathustra overcomes his pity for the higher men and leaves them behind without even bidding them adieu. Perhaps a central purpose of the whole book is to purge the psyche of every potential Zarathustra of the temptation to minister to any form of piety? On close examination, even Parts I–III already hint at a considerable distance between

Zarathustra's speeches and his inner convictions. As the hunchback in Part II unmistakably intimates, Zarathustra says one thing to his disciples and something quite different to himself.

The contemporary world has had its share of Nietzscheans—from Peter Gast to Ernst Bertram as well as other members of the Stefan George Circle; from fascist leader Gabrielle d'Annunzio to Protestant pastors Albert Kalthoff and Max Maurenbrecher to socialist-anarchist Gustav Landauer; from expressionist Gottfried Benn (prior to 1933) to postmodernists such as Michel Foucault and Georges Bataille[4]—notwithstanding the deeply paradoxical character of Nietzsche's doctrines. The disciples and imitators have all failed to take due note of his many warnings about discipleship: "Verily," says Zarathustra to his flock, "I counsel you: go away from me and resist Zarathustra! . . . Perhaps he deceived you. The man of knowledge must not only love his enemies but also be able to hate his friends. One repays a teacher badly if one always remains nothing but a pupil. . . . You are my believers—but what matter all believers. . . . All faith amounts to so little. Now I bid you to lose me and find yourselves." Nor have they heeded an absolutely crucial passage (cited above in chapter 3) in Nietzsche's *Antichrist* (54): "One should not be misled: great minds are skeptics. Zarathustra is a skeptic. . . . Convictions are prisons. . . . The man of faith, the 'believer,' of every kind, is necessarily a dependent man . . ." Regarding spiritual independence, Nietzsche goes so far as to declare openly, in *The Genealogy of Morals*, that it is better to will the nothing than not will, an outrageously bold and exaggerated restatement of Socratic impiety that, to say the least, cannot be defended without careful qualification. At any rate, notwithstanding his esotericism, Nietzsche wishes to lead the most promising human beings from the dark cave of faith into the natural light of philosophic freedom.

Escaping the bonds of faith does not come easily even for the most resolute. Family, fatherland, and friends all have their siren songs and, for apostates, severe sanctions. No less seductively, in our time, even philosophy can appear on the scene draped in the robes of venerable tradition. (*Beyond Good and Evil* appropriately begins with an attack "On the Prejudices of the Philosophers" that explicitly challenges the possibility and legitimacy of the will to truth.) Nietzsche urges the best of the youth to hearken to nature, to tear off those robes and cast them aside, to enjoy the sweet pleasures of philosophy naked and in the flesh—not as a rape, but with philosophic *eros* as a most willing partner.

No ethical rule or metaphysical doctrine, then, but only the life of philosophy matters to Nietzsche in the end. His whole "philosophy" of will to power and eternal return aims to shake to the eye teeth the self-evidence of a rationalistic, philosophic approach—and thus to make genuine, self-questioning love of wisdom, à la Plato, possible again. The Nietzschean images of nobility derive their pedagogical necessity from the manifest inadequacies of bourgeois existence and from the irrepressible longings of the great-souled young. If those images are lies, then they are noble lies in the Platonic-Socratic double sense that they challenge the young to ascend to their highest capacities and simultaneously reflect basic verities about human nature. The latter include the enduring truths that striving to overcome ourselves remains essential to our humanity and that for the human being in full bloom the unexamined life would not be worth living. In the best case, the more fully one understands these truths and acts accordingly, the deeper one's joy may grow over the opportunities that life brings ("We would consider every day wasted," remarks Zarathustra, "in which we had not danced at least once. And we would consider every truth false that was not followed by at least one laugh."); and the more willing one may become, were it possible, to relive one's whole life again, unchanged, in the future.

NOTES

1. See Löwith, *Nietzsche's Philosophy of the Eternal Recurrence*.

2. *Nietzsche*, trans. David Farrell Krell, Vol. 1: *The Will to Power as Art* (San Francisco: Harper and Row, 1979); Vol. 2: *The Eternal Return* (San Francisco: Harper and Row, 1984); Vol. 3: *The Will to Power as Knowledge and Metaphysics* (San Francisco: Harper and Row, 1986); Vol. 4: *Nihilism* (San Francisco: Harper and Row, 1982).

3. "The Drama of Zarathustra," pp. 220–31.

4. For an example of a current American Nietzschean whose books amply merit perusal, see Lawrence Lampert, *Nietzsche's Teaching: An Interpretation of* Thus Spoke Zarathustra (New Haven, Conn.: Yale University Press, 1986); *Nietzsche and Modern Times* (New Haven, Conn., Yale University Press, 1993); and *Leo Strauss and Nietzsche* (Chicago: University of Chicago Press, 1996).

Index

Socrates, xi, 1, 5, 6, 9, 13, 14, 15,
18, 21, 31, 36, 56–57, 64–66,
68, 69–70, 71, 73, 78, 90–91,
97–98, 102–3, 107, 109, 111,
114, 116, 118, 126, 127
Sophocles, 19–20
Spinoza, Baruch, 23, 27–28, 32,
39, 49
Stendhal: see Beyle
Stoics, 33, 49, 72
Strauss, Leo, xiii, 3, 70, 76, 77,
80, 119, 120, 122, 127

Vikings, 175
Volkmann-Schluck, Karl-Heinz, 119

Voltaire: see Francois Marie
Arouet

Xanthippe, 64
Xenophon, 70, 78

Wagner, Richard, 9, 116
Wotan, 115

Zarathustra, xii, 1, 4, 7, 8, 11, 12,
20, 25, 29, 32, 39, 54, 62–63,
67, 68, 73, 74, 75, 76, 77–78,
79–80, 86–88, 93, 94, 95, 104,
111, 117–18, 119, 120, 125–26,
127

About the Author

J Harvey Lomax is Associate Professor of Political Science at the University of Memphis. He is the translator of Karl Löwith's *Nietzsche's Philosophy of the Eternal Recurrence of the Same* (1997).